A Second
CHANCE

Grace for the Broken

D1512215

Keith A. Battle

DISCLAIMER

The advice and strategies given in this book may not be suitable for every situation. This work is sold with the understanding that the author and publisher are not engaged in rendering psychological, legal, accounting, or other professional services. Neither the author nor the publisher shall be liable for damages arising here from. The fact that an organization or website is referred to in this book as a citation or a potential source of further information does not mean that the author or the publisher endorses the information that the organization or website may provide or recommendations it may make. Furthermore, readers should be aware that Internet websites listed in this book may have changed or disappeared between when this book was written and when it is read.

ENDORSEMENTS

In my book *A Setback Is a Setup for a Comeback,* I share that some setbacks in life are thrust upon you, while others are self-made setbacks! Either way, it is critical that you know you can get a second chance to comeback bigger and better. Keith Battle shares powerful tips in this book to help you learn and grow no matter how the setback occurred. I highly recommend you read this book, re-read it, and then share it with people in your network who need to not only do better but also need to be better! You'll be glad you did!"
—**Dr. Willie Jolley—Best Selling Author of** *A Setback Is a Setup for a Comeback* **and** *An Attitude of Excellence*

This memoir from a mentor's heart is an essential read for ministry leaders at every level to protect the ministry God has given to them. *A Second Chance* helps leaders avoid falling and gives guidance to those who have fallen. This book is a win-win for churches and leaders everywhere.
—**Douglas Weiss, PhD, Psychologist, Executive Director of Heart to Heart Counseling Center, Author, and Conference Speaker**

Keith Battle quickly admits his own brokenness. He clearly understands the cracks so skillfully hidden in each of our hearts. His practical wisdom sensitively bridges the gap between Bible-based theology and real-world insight.
—**Bobb Biehl, Executive Mentor**

It is the uncommon leader who lifts up the window shade and allows you a peek at their soul—becoming vulnerable about their brokenness. Keith's transparency is deeply refreshing and extremely rare at his level of leadership as a pastor. I only intended to read the first chapter and write my endorsement—not so. *A Second Chance* is a page-turner, brimming with hope as it offers a plan to rebuild your broken world built on God's foundation of grace.

—Dr. Johnny Parker, Leadership Consultant, Certified Professional Counselor, Executive Coach, and Author of *Renovating Your Marriage Room by Room.*

ACKNOWLEDGMENTS

Above all, I thank my God and my Lord Savior Jesus Christ, whose grace is *amazing* and whose love is relentless. Thank You, Father, for another chance.

To my precious treasure, my wife Vicki. Your love for me is a reflection of God's love. I am so much better because of you. I cherish you. Thank you for believing in me before I did.

To my children, Asha, Asa, and Kendall, let the record state that I love you all more than I'm able to express. Thanks for not giving up on me as I continue to learn to be a better dad.

To my pastor, John K. Jenkins, Sr. and his wife, Trina. You two have covered Vicki and me in a priceless way. Thanks for your counsel, patience, support, blessing, and unconditional love.

To Barry Levy, thank you for helping me to discover me.

To my Circle of Peers in my Tuesday Small Group, thanks, brothers, for walking this journey with me. Thanks to each of you for standing tall and broken at the same time.

And to my Zion Church Family in Landover, Maryland; Woodbridge, Virginia; Fort Washington, Maryland; and those connected with us through our Internet campuses across the world. Thanks for loving and laughing and living with me. Leading and serving you guys has taught me so much. Thanks for your patience with me as I have walked, stumbled, fallen, and stood back up, all in front of you. It's a privilege to be your pastor.

TABLE OF CONTENTS

INTRODUCTION

None of us grow up planning to fail, particularly those of us who aspire to be leaders. We all see ourselves succeeding and leading in our respective fields. We see ourselves making the university, the company, the department, the church, or the team better than it's ever been before. We see ourselves breaking records for growth, revenue, and market share. We see ourselves in board meetings, mulling over big decisions for expansion and mergers and new locations and additional staff and bonuses.

But we *rarely* see ourselves failing; at least not *morally*. We never see ourselves having to apologize to our constituents, colleagues, direct reports, students, faculty, board, and members for making poor choices in our personal or professional life—or both. We never imagined the deafening sound of the *thud* that accompanies the fall of a leader or the embarrassment that comes with knowing that so many people who depended on you to be solid and honorable and wise are now aware that you were foolish and reckless and prideful and destructive.

When leaders fall, the aftershocks and quaking in their wake continues for days and weeks and months and even years. It's the price that the leader and others around them must pay for their failure. Let me be clear up front; I'm not writing this book as a pristine leader with an unblemished record, trying to dissuade other more *impressionable* leaders to walk the sacred path that I've walked—far from it.

I write this book as a leader who still has the fragrance of failure in my garments and as one who everyday marvels that God in His amazing grace has allowed me to once again lead even after failure. I write this book as a leader who has gone through a journey of failure and recovery that I will share with you with all of the transparency that God would permit me to share without dragging others, who deserve their privacy, through the mud of my murky road. Might I add that I also am not writing this book as a victim nor do I write it as a hero; rather, I write it from one broken soul to another with the hope that you may experience the same grace that I've experienced.

If you are holding this book with a quivering hand and a disturbed soul because you have plunged shamefully into an abyss of failure, the pages in this book are my life-line to you. I care deeply about your future and I'm prayerful that in this book you will find your way safely out of the gulf of your despair into a stable and fruitful future.

Keith Battle

CHAPTER 1

WHY A SECOND CHANCE?

I'm not really sure I can answer the question as to why God gives people like me second chances and even third chances, and chance after chance after chance for that matter. I *do* know that He's not like humans because *our* philosophy is, "If you fool me once, shame on you. But if you fool me twice, shame on me." In fact, we think it *prudent* not to give people second chances when they've burned us before, and I believe that is a wise approach to interpersonal dealings. But with God, there is no shame in His forgiveness and giving of second chances because He's never fooled by our failures.

You see, one of the attributes of God is His omniscience, which means He knows *everything.* Part of his knowledge acumen is His *foreknowledge,* which means He knows things before they happen. God doesn't have to wait for something to happen to experience it because He's not bound by time. He is above and beyond time, yet He chooses to operate in the limitations of time. Meanwhile, He can see everything from eternity past to infinity future at the same time.

Therefore, there is nothing that you or I could ever do that would surprise God and make Him second-guess His decision to choose us to lead. Indeed, He knew the failures, sins, and mistakes that we would make when He first picked us and gifted us with leadership abilities. So actually, God didn't give me a second chance when I failed, He gave me a second chance when He chose me, knowing ahead of time that failure was a part of a future that I had not yet lived. That blesses me, and I hope it blesses you, too. Allow me to also add to this fact that not only is God not surprised by our failures, but He doesn't love us any less because of them, either.

So I pray that this book will serve as a recovery map for those of us who have failed and fallen as leaders, because you may indeed be a better leader now that you've failed, than you were before your fall. Let me explain.

Humpty Dumpty Leaders

A minister friend of mine, with whom I enjoy periodic dialogue once shared with me an interesting take on the story of Humpty Dumpty that I had never heard before.

In case you don't know the story, permit me to recite it here:

> Humpty Dumpty sat on a wall,
> Humpty Dumpty had a great fall,
> And all the King's Horses, and all the King's Men,
> Couldn't put Humpty together again.

My friend said to me, "Keith, has it ever dawned on you that Humpty was a man of authority? That's why he was sitting on the wall. And he must have been a man of great affluence as well because when he fell, no expense was spared to rescue, repair, and restore him. (*All* the Kings Horses, and *all* the King's Men were rushed to the scene.) But Keith, two great things happened in Mr. Dumpty's life. The first is that he fell. It *broke* him and *humbled* him. The second is that he *remained in that broken and humbled state.*"

Humpty Dumpty's fall and the irreparable injuries that he incurred were *both blessings* because, in the words of author Dan B. Allender, Humpty can "lead with a limp." You see, my friend, although I have "recovered" from my failure as a leader, and God has restored me to lead again, what has not changed is how *broken and humble* I am as a result of my fall. In fact, I live in this dichotomous paradigm all of the time, wherein on the one hand I'm so sorry that I hurt so many people and let so many people down, but on the other hand, I'm so glad that I fell off that wall of pride and self-righteousness. It was indeed the greatest plunge of my life. I'm so glad that my failure remains fresh in my mind every day, reminding me of what a *privilege* it is for me to lead, and not a *right*.

Broken Vessels and Bright Lights

When Vicki and I first got married, one of our wedding gifts was two green nightstand lamps. They were kind of trendy as the lightbulbs were covered with a forest green colored glass that gave a cool tint to the light in the room. Unfortunately, I accidentally knocked the one on my nightstand on the floor one day, and it cracked open the green colored glass covering the lightbulb. The lamp remained operable and pretty much intact; there was just an embarrassing hole in the lightbulb cover. So to hide this deficiency from guests who would come over to visit our very humble dwelling, we simply turned the lamp around so that the hole wasn't visible. However, as time went on, I noticed something about that particular broken, but functional lamp. From time to time, when Vicki and I were home alone, I would turn the lamp in a direction where the hole was facing me because if I was reading a book, the added brightness made it easier to read. I also noticed that if I ever needed to see something in the direction of our closet that was to the left of our bed, I would turn the opening of the lamp in that direction, as well, because it illuminated the area more. It was sort-of like a gigantic flashlight in those instances.

So what I discovered was that although we had two lamps in the room, one had the potential to give us more light than the other because its cover was broken. And that broken "vessel" produced a brighter light. My fall from my wall of pseudo-perfection and pride caused me to be broken, but the blessing is that since God has allowed my brokenness to remain, I believe more of His glorious light is able to shine through my life. And for that I'm grateful.

Dr. Crawford Loritts once said, "A leader who's not broken will always end up breaking people." I know that from experience. I'm a much safer leader, humbled and broken, than I was when I thought I had it all together.

CHAPTER 2

THE FALL

All leaders who fail inevitably have a blind spot somewhere in their lives that makes them vulnerable but unaware of their vulnerability. For me it was an *insatiable ambition*. I have always longed to be the best and the greatest in everything that I've attempted to do. I have always been very competitive for as long as I can remember. I never wanted to lose and always struggled with it when it happened. My ambition wasn't about being *one* of the best in my generation. That would've been too modest.

My ambition was to be *the greatest* to ever do what I did in the history of humankind. Some of you reading this can relate. That's why you lead, because you *have* to. It's just who you are. Ambition is something that fuels us as leaders. Now ambition alone is not a bad thing. I believe it's necessary to build great institutions and organizations. However, when that ambition is insatiable, it can lead to recklessness.

That's the kind of ambition that drove me to begin making some decisions in the fall of 2011 that would set me up for the painful descent from my "wall." Let me give you the background to my descent.

Multi-Sites or Bust

Our church had raised about $2.2 million in capital campaign funds with the goal of trying to secure our own facility. This was exciting on the one hand because in the eleven-year history of our church at that time, we had never owned any real estate. We were excited to be raising money with the goal of property ownership. The problem is, we were already reaching about 2,500 people in person at our weekend services at our Landover, Maryland campus. It would cost us about $30 million in land and construction costs to secure and build the kind of facility that would house a church of our size. This meant we would need to raise another $8 million before we could get a bank to invest that kind of money in us.

This was heartbreaking; it took us several years and much sacrifice to raise the $2.2 million. There's no way we could raise another $8 million! I'd be old and gray by the time that happened. Therefore, I decided instead of continuing to try to *purchase* a facility where we'd have our church, we'd *lease* and build-out several smaller facilities in different areas for what I estimated would cost us about $500,000 in start-up costs per campus, or location. Thus, we would be a multi-site church with several campuses. If we could get these campuses up and running for $500k or less, we could launch four new campuses.

I ambitiously challenged my leadership team and staff to launch new campuses with this $2.2 million—that we couldn't really do anything with because the money was restricted solely for land or property acquisition. I sought legal advice on the matter and was instructed that if we wanted to use this designated income for something other than the purpose for which it was given, I would have to go back to the congregation and explain the reason for the change and give anyone who had contributed to the capital campaign the option of receiving a refund on their donations if they didn't agree with the new direction and intended use of the funds. I went before the congregation with a compelling vision that Zion Church was a movement, not a monument. We couldn't afford to erect one huge facility somewhere; instead we would do these economically savvy campuses and be able to reach people in many locations.

To my delight, out of the $2.2 million in donations, we only had about $40,000 worth of refund requests. In fact, we were blessed to have one of our newer members give a one-time donation of $425,000 to support our vision because she was so happy with what we were doing, especially for the poor in our communities. And that gift in particular was a huge motivator for me to move forward with my audacious plans, partly because I was convinced that her one gift would almost finance an entire new campus for us. So with that, we moved forward.

We started our first campus in Woodbridge, Virginia, and before that campus was up and running, we began hiring staff to launch a campus in Waldorf, Maryland. And before I even signed a lease for the campus in Waldorf, Maryland (more about that in a moment), we began looking to launch a campus in Columbia, Maryland, as well as in Washington, DC.

Poor Calculations

Our staff at the time was about nineteen people, and it took us twelve years to hire that many people. But because we needed additional personnel to manage and lead this huge undertaking, I added another twenty persons to our full-time staff in a four-month period, which brought our full-time staff from nineteen to thirty-nine. That is not to mention additional part-time staff and contractors who were also added to our payroll during this time.

So, not only did I double our salaries with the new hires, to make matters worse for us organizationally, several of the people that we hired were paid salaries by Zion Church comparable to the jobs that they were leaving in spite of the fact that the salaries were way over what would be reasonable compensation for a ministry of our size. We were now strapped with terribly exorbitant salaries with the hopes of executing this ambitious mission.

Moreover, while the significant increase of our staff more than doubled our expenses, our income remained the same. That was something that I hadn't thoroughly calculated; however, I was so confident that my brilliant plan would work that I believed that these four new campuses would be up and running so quickly that they would be generating revenue from offerings that would more than cover all of our outlay. Meanwhile we were essentially paying these new salaries out of that rapidly diminishing $2.6-million pot of cash (including the large donor gift) because by now we had more than shattered the 10 percent margin that we had operated on for years, leading up to this point. So we were already in a mini-financial crisis mode, but I was in the words of the late ESPN Sports Analyst Stuart Scott, "As cool as the other side of the pillow" because I was in a hyper-ambitious and driven state.

In addition to the additional staff and contractor costs associated with this huge endeavor, because we were now going to be a multiple-site church, using video recording or streaming from our Landover location to show at these new venues, it was important that we upgrade all of the technology on the Landover campus in order to increase the quality of the experience that we would have at each location. This was about a $900,000 audio-visual (A/V) upgrade, including a new state-of-the art sound system with all new digital equipment, swapping out the analog equipment that was currently in place. The purchase of four new high-definition, television-quality cameras, six new flat-screen televisions in the main sanctuary, and other technology enhancements. Although this work and the payments were staggered, this bill also had to come from the $2.6-million pot of cash. That was something else that I hadn't anticipated.

In the meantime, the movement continued with the start of our Woodbridge, Virginia campus with a huge outreach and carnival in the community. The startup cost for this campus was just south of $500,000 to cover the costs for all of the A/V and other equipment necessary to begin having church in that area. And of course, that too, came out of the $2.6-million pot of cash, which I actually *did* anticipate. However, the thing that I hadn't calculated in all of my ambition was the fact that the cost to *maintain* this new fully-functioning, multi-staffed location wouldn't be even close to covered by the meager offerings that came in during the early stages of the church. So the Zion Woodbridge Campus was upside down by *thousands* of dollars every single week, requiring a subsidy of an additional over $300,000 its first year. And guess where that money was coming from? So needless to say, Zion Church was hemorrhaging financially at this point, and I wish that I could tell you that I had the sobriety of thought and humility of character to stop the bleeding, but things would actually get worse.

In spite of repeated warnings from my C.F.O. and questions and concerns from other competent leaders around me, I continued to forge ahead. To say the least, at this point in my life and leadership, I wasn't making sound decisions with others in mind. Instead, I was making reckless, ambitious, self-centered choices, with only myself and what I wanted in mind. To make matters worse, while we were literally in the midst of a financial free fall, I made an even more reckless decision and signed a ten-year, $2.3-million lease agreement on a property in Waldorf, Maryland. This was going to be an additional campus where we would expand our reach to impact more lives. However, this facility would need $1 million worth of tenant improvements and renovations before we could even begin to have worship services in there. I signed the lease, assuming that the landlord would pay for 100 percent of the $1-million build-out cost, and then roll those costs into the ten-year lease. Unfortunately, I never verified that assumption in writing before signing the lease, only later to find out that the owner agreed to only *split* the construction costs 50–50 with us, which meant we were on the hook for an additional $500,000 in construction costs, not including the additional hundreds of thousands of dollars in A/V costs, and so forth, that we knew we'd have to pay just to get that campus up and running. Of course, these expenses *also* would be coming out of that now fiscally anemic $2.6-million pot of cash.

In addition to that, we also had three full-time staff members assigned to the Waldorf campus and on payroll before we began construction on the building, which of course, was also milking our rapidly shrinking cash reserves. I won't bore you with all of the other details of this embarrassing period of my life and leadership. I think the picture is sad enough. But I will say that fortunately, it all came to a screeching halt before we moved ahead with the Columbia, Maryland campus, for which we were aggressively looking for a facility, as well as a campus in Washington, DC. My reckless decisions that I was hiding from my mentor and pastor were shamefully exposed, and he immediately intervened and put me on a discipline process that saved my life, my marriage, my family, and my ministry. I was placed on sabbatical for nearly four months while I received extensive counseling.

Meanwhile, the Waldorf campus project had to be aborted. Many families were negatively impacted. The morale of our church was at an all-time low. Humpty Dumpty had a great fall.

The Cataclysmic Damage and Ripple Effect

One of the greatest burdens of responsibility on a leader is the fact that their influence, good or bad, affects all of those in their wake. So when they make good and great decisions, it benefits all who are a part of their following. But when they make poor or immoral decisions the fallout is felt on a large scale. In January 2013, after placing the church in a financial position that could have closed our doors, seventeen people on our staff either resigned or were terminated because of my reckless ambition and poor decision-making. Many of these people had quit their secure jobs in other places and industries to come and work for Zion Church, and most of them couldn't get their old jobs back. Some of them are still reeling from the financial impact of their termination even at the time of the writing of this book, trying to regain their financial footing after such a devastating blow. And even the twenty-two of us who remained on staff, along with many of the contractors as well, took pay cuts and lost benefits to try to stabilize our church financially.

It was a nightmare. People were demoralized. For many, their hope and trust in church, and certainly in me, was justifiably gone. Humpty Dumpty had fallen. And no one ever talks about all the people that were crushed that he landed on. *Fortune Magazine* estimates that "Companies experience an average shareholder loss of $226 Million in the three days after the announcement of a CEO indiscretion"[1]

The impact of leadership failure is very difficult to quantify, but we know the damage is massive. For each of the people and families that I hurt, I am truly sorry. I am a better person today, but I will never cease to be sorry for who I was and the pain that I caused many because of it. For some of those who had been released, we have been able to restore them to their jobs at Zion Church again over the last four years. We've done it without violating our margin policy. In fact, our margin is much higher than 10 percent these days.

Meanwhile, others, I'm sure, have no interest in returning to a place of such disappointment and leadership failure. For that I am saddened and sorrowful, but even more so, I am repentant. We've been able to help others with financial support or even shelter for a season. Others we've hired again as contractors. Additionally, all who were released or resigned received as generous a severance package as we could provide given the circumstances. It's still a cloud that I'm not sure will ever lift from our church's history or from my leadership. I think that's a good thing because it serves as a reminder of how delicate a stewardship leadership really is.

CHAPTER 3

THE ANATOMY OF A FALL

I wrote this book with people, leaders especially, in mind who've had embarrassing failures, some devastatingly public and some that were mercifully private in nature. I wrote it because I believe there is a road map, to climb out of the abyss of moral failure, regardless of what that failure is. God's grace is amazing. Allow me to share the other side of my story. As sad as that time was in 2011 and 2012 for me, as well as so many people affected by my failures, at the same time so many blessings have come as a result of it. For one, my own sense of self-awareness is so much more heightened now. I really understand myself better and what makes me think and do the things that I do. And although that might seem trivial on the surface, it is actually critically important for us as leaders to be self-aware because a lot of our leadership prowess is instinctive. Leaders like me, especially, tend to be very spontaneous, and therefore we are not always aware of what's going on internally that's driving our behavior and decisions.

What failing has done for me has given me the time and space to self-reflect enough to know how I ended up where I was. I think that is very crucial because in my humble opinion, I think what may be an even greater tragedy than the widespread pain and trauma associated with a leader's failure and fall is if that leader at some point *returns* to a leadership role without knowing why they fell. "Blind" mistakes are bound to be repeated. So if you have experienced some kind of moral, financial, spiritual, public, or private failure as a leader, discovering how that failure unfolded in your life is going to be essential to you maximizing your *second chance.* Allow me to show you how I learned to discover the pathology of my own failure and give you some tools that can help you discover your own journey downward.

The Film Room

I love watching sports and I would consider myself a pretty avid fan of several sports. One of the keys to victory in the world of sports, whether it's basketball, football, or boxing, is time spent in the *film room*. The film room is where motion pictures of previous games and matches are viewed with the highest level of scrutiny. Film tape can be played at super-slow-motion speed to assure that every detail is examined. It is in the film room that the best athletes and coaches study their opponent's tendencies and study ways to defend against their opponent and effective ways to score against their opponent. It's also in the film room where your own mistakes are pointed out, and missteps are clearly seen. It's where poor techniques and bad decision-making is highlighted. These failures are not pointed out to beat up the one who failed but to strengthen their performance in the future.

Anytime leaders fall, they *must* go into the film room and unpack the process by which their demise came about. This is *critical* for their future success. For me, that process has been invaluable. I have spent countless hours in the film room of counseling (more about this and other support groups that a fallen leader needs in Chapter 5). I have spent tireless hours in prayer and study and self-examination. During the time of my four-month disciplinary sabbatical, I invested each day working tirelessly to not only get better as a person but also to evaluate what was unknowingly broken within me that caused me to make such poor, self-centered, reckless decisions. I treated my recovery work as a fallen leader like a full-time job. Overcoming leadership failure is not easy, but it's certainly not impossible. What I discovered in the "film room" is that my public failure was born out of a private deterioration that began long before I failed.

Dangerous Disconnections

I had become a leader, who, over a period of time, began relying more on my talents and instincts than I did on God. My journey as a leader of the church that I started was one that was saturated in prayer and spiritual focus from the beginning. I had no idea what I was doing, and I desperately needed God at every stage in the early days of Zion Church's formation, if for no other reason than the fact that I just wanted God to insure that I didn't make a fool of myself. I sincerely remember being quite desperate for God and His wisdom and guidance and direction in my life. I remember not just kneeling in prayer, but literally laying on the floor with my face on the ground, pleading with Him to guide me and bless Zion Church.

In fact, many "veteran" Zion Church members often speak of the Mercantile Lane days. What they're referring to is the time when we were renting out space in an office park on Mercantile Lane in Largo, Maryland. In that little place, we as a congregation were hungry for God. However, when I think about 2011, I can remember going days without really connecting with God in formal times of prayer and meditation. And those times of desperation for God were long gone, partly because by now we were "experts" at this thing. We were seeing thousands of people every weekend, and we put on great productions each week. We had great videos, creative sermons, and entertaining music all threaded together like a beautifully arranged performance each week.

But *I* know that it was all lacking the life and power of God. Primarily because *I* was. When I disconnected from God, it was only a matter of time before my own human ability and strength would face levels that I was ill-equipped to handle properly. Not only was I disconnected from God, but as I sat for days in my own "film room" during my sabbatical, I realized that I was even more disconnected at home. My beautiful wife Vicki and my three children would see me at home, but I wasn't really *engaged* with them. I provided financially for them and I did that pretty well, but as far as being *"present"* at home and *fully aware* of what was going on in their lives and engaged in their lives, I was as distant as I had ever been before. Vicki and I rarely went on dates, rarely sharing our feelings with each other. We didn't speak words of praise and adoration to each other, and we weren't praying together. It's not like those were things she was unwilling to do. Those things weren't happening because I was more interested in the church I was building, when ironically, it wasn't really mine to build in the first place.

Meanwhile, Vicki and I were basically roommates, managing our household, and raising children together, and because she rarely if ever complains,

I continued to allow our lives to drift apart. Since I wasn't winning at home in my marriage, I did what so many leaders do in those situations, we turn our businesses, companies, or ministries into our mistresses, and we spend more and more time with them. The thinking is, if I'm not a great husband, at least I'm a great company president, or CEO, or pastor. And so I began to medicate the pain that I was feeling regarding the dissatisfaction at home with injections of success at Church. Since I didn't have a very close relationship with my kids, instead of working on that, I accepted the mediocrity of those relationships and worked on building more of a family environment at work. I was closer to my staff than I was to my own family.

Then there was a third disconnect that was critical to my demise, and it was a disconnect from the spiritual authority and mentor in my life; my pastor. I believe every pastor *needs* a pastor and I have had one throughout my year's as a pastor, but began to withdraw myself from that relationship. I subtly distanced myself from my pastor because I knew that if he knew how disconnected I was from God, and from Vicki and my children, that he would call me to the carpet on it. And I didn't want to be accountable; I wanted to be successful. How could I be successful if I put all of my attention into my marriage and children? I mean, how am I supposed to build this mega-organization, if I'm doing all of this family stuff. My thinking was, "Hey, my family's cool. Everybody's basically okay. Besides, this is *God's* work, I'm engaging in. I'm changing lives and touching the world."

I also didn't want my pastor to know how reckless I was when it came to our church's finances for it was he who had taught me years earlier to always operate with a financial margin. He modeled that for me, and we followed in his footsteps as a church until 2011 when I began to compromise that conviction to satisfy my ambition and drive. So I was at a point in my life when all of my critical relationships were being neglected. I wasn't close to God. I was distant from Vicki and my children, and I was ducking and dodging my pastor. Any leader who is hiding is either in trouble or not far from trouble.

If you're a leader and you're in what I'll call this drifting phase that precedes moral failure and you know that you're not connected in a healthy way with your spouse, your children, or your spiritual authority or someone that holds you accountable, I *plead* with you, desperately cry out for help and run back to those valuable and protecting relationships because there is nothing good on the other side of the street no matter how enticing or alluring it may be. The price is far higher than you want to pay.

The Value of the Film Room

If you're a leader and you've had a moral failure, or if you're offering loving counsel and support to someone who has fallen, one of the greatest gifts that the fallen leader can receive is the gift of discovering the key elements that led to their demise. This probing is essential, not for the sake of embarrassment, but for the sake of future empowerment. Pretend that I'm a quarterback and I don't know why I got sacked and fumbled. If I'm ever back in the game and under center again, I may not recognize the blitz that blind-sided me before. Likewise when it comes to certain levels of leadership, *one fall* and subsequent recovery is possible, so much so, that the leader can exceed the level of leadership that he fell from. Albeit if a leader falls the same way twice, he will more than likely never ascend to that level of leadership again. That's the tragic reality of the narrow realm of leadership expectations and responsibilities.

The reason why this book is called *A Second* Chance and not *Chance after Chance* is because leaders are rarely allowed to make the same catastrophic mistake twice and continue at their level of leadership. To whom much is given, much is required. What the leader gets who has failed terribly *once* and *recovered* is the title, "The Guy who Made the Most of a Second Chance." What the leader gets who has committed the same terrible failure more than once is a lifetime support or advisory role somewhere, or a leadership role on a much smaller scale, and a title, such as:

The Guy who Can't Keep His Hand Out of the Cookie Jar
The Gal who Can't Keep Her Skirt Down
The Guy who Can't Get Off of the Pipe
The Gal who Can't Stay Off of the Bottle
The Guy who Can't Stay Away from Slot Machines and Crap Tables

They may say he's a great guy, smart as a whip, but he never got that personal stuff under control. And on and on it goes.

There may in some cases be a rare occasion of grace for the leader who had *two different categories* of public failure. Maybe the first time he succumbed to an illicit relationship, and the second time, years later, he was pulled over for driving under the influence. That leader *may* get grace. But if he ever *repeats* the same public failure twice, stick a fork in him; he's done. Leadership is not baseball. In leadership, two strikes, and you're out. Usually you'd have to outlive several generations and Google search engines to ever return to the level of leadership that you struck out at. Nevertheless, I have good news for those whom *people* may have given up on in Chapter 6. God specializes in recalls.

The Road to Perdition

When a leader falls into an extramarital affair or adultery or other sexually addictive behavior or when a leader falls into a pattern of alcohol or substance abuse or when a leader falls into the temptation of pilfering company or charitable funds their way illegitimately or maybe a leader was finally exposed for having a gambling addiction that caused them to lose their home, their car, and their family, the road can be as long and varied as each particular individual. Not one size fits all.

But generally speaking, a leader whose responsibility is to lead an organization with moral integrity doesn't just suddenly find themselves in the bed with another person or behind bars for some other illicit failure. It's a process. Now although each plunge takes a different route and happens at a different pace, given each particular leader's circumstances, they all have similarities. For the sake of simplicity, I'll address the fall that has been more and more common among leaders, and that is the fall into an inappropriate sexual relationship.

Typically this "fall" starts with the combination of an unhealthy *detachment* from their spouse and an unhealthy *attachment* to their career. Many affairs begin covertly under the veil of hard work and long hours. The harder the work and the longer the hours and the greater the demands, the less of themselves leaders have for their spouses and even for their children. Indeed you cannot burn a candle at both ends without the candle suffering enormous burnout. So subsequently, the leader uses the home for recovery so that they will have their best energy, best ideas, best creativity, best prayers, and best conversations for work. That leaves the people at home that they've been given to love with leftover energy, day-old ideas, stale creativity, molding prayers, and spoiled conversations.

Meanwhile of course, everybody at work think they are hot to trot, especially the person they work the closest to. And everybody at work sees them at their very best. And when they come home from a day of praise and adoration and three rounds of "For he's a Jolly-Good Fellow, which nobody can deny," and the garbage awaits him and a lawn that needs cutting and a wife who is too tired to talk at all, much less praise him or have sexual intimacy with him, he's on his way to a place where he'd vowed he'd never go. Now these inappropriate relationships can take years to develop and materialize. They often start in the mind and heart first. In other words, they become a part of an individual's fantasy world before they become a part of their reality.

But if something's not done to correct the disconnect at home and the hard wiring and strengthening of the connection at work or wherever the extra relationship is, then the leader is heading down a slippery slope that's invisible but deadly. Eventually, the leader who converses less and less with their spouse will have more and more conversations with their "interest" because they're so *easy* to talk with. They *"get"* each other. They respect each other. They have time for each other. And quite frankly because they *both* are often lonely in their marriages (if the person of interest is married), they kind of feel like they deserve each other.

Entitlement may be the biggest motivator to the fall of a leader. The thinking that is their downfall is "I work hard. I help a lot of people. I have a lot of success. I bring in a lot of money to this organization. I deserve to have some pleasure and to reap some rewards for my labor that are not necessarily a part of my salary or benefit package." So conversations go beyond work to interests. And this leads to extended time together, even time outside of work. That often leads to a strong sexual tension or *attraction* that grows between the two people that if not shut down is headed for big, big trouble.

At this point, the leader can either desperately reach out for accountability and help, making the tough call to get help in their marriage and to get away from the person, or they can keep going down this slippery slope into an abyss of shame and guilt and dangerous pleasure. Too often that happens. Now the relationship has moved into a level of secrecy. The meetings and conversations are more dominated by personal things than they are about business or curriculum or budgets or building lives. Secret plans of connections are made. Risk management is set in place. The agenda is no longer "Will we go too far, but when and how will we pull off what was once unthinkable?"

During this time, leaders live in a very duplicitous place. For on the one hand they will try their best to live their life at home and work with as much normalcy as possible, but what they will work hard to mask and keep undisclosed is the growing, monstrous, erotic, passionate relationship that has grown out of control. Intimacy with the spouse is now impossible because there is no intimacy if you can't see into me. And you cannot see into me if I'm hiding a huge part of my heart and soul from you. And in addition, because of all that's at stake, the leader is now hiding from their friends and other family members and colleagues, who once held them accountable for living with integrity.

They have to *act* like things are okay and cool when they're not because not only are they now working extremely hard to cover their tracks and save their job and reputation and the integrity of their organization, but they're also working hard to *protect* their new drug of choice because, as wrong as it is, it is medicating the pain and the emptiness in their life that comes from having empty personal relationships. The guilt and shame and secrecy and cover-ups and the fear and anxiety and the internal civil war that's happening in their soul as they live with the ongoing conflict of being happy with a relationship that's totally wrong, makes this kind of relationship terribly taxing on the people involved, and it also hurts their productivity and the quality of their professional decision making as well, because they're "high" a lot of times and not sober. Whether it's drugs, money, alcohol, or illicit sex, all of it is an attempt to medicate the pain of our reality with the pleasure of the fantasy world we've developed.

The Power of Shame

Author and counselor Stephen Arterburn writes profoundly about the subject of shame in a person's life who has been clutched by sexual sin in particular:

> "I think shame is one of the more powerful triggers to bring a man back into lust and unfaithfulness. It makes us feel unworthy of God's love or the love of a spouse. So in our secrecy, isolation, and pain, when we feel like we don't deserve the taste of transformation we have experienced, we jump right back into the cycle that created the shame in the first place.
>
> Over the years I have made a few discoveries that have helped me in my own journey toward wholeness and healing. One of those discoveries is the power of shame. Shame is the

cancer that can completely eat away a soul. It is most likely what kept you from getting help long ago. You probably believed that the shame of being known and openly dealing with your problem was greater than the shame of leading a double life full of secrets and duplicity. Shame kept you in the problem for other reasons too. Every time that shame started to overwhelm you and drive you toward the worst of who you had become, you had an instant fix for the feeling. You acted out or 'acted in,' filling your mind with the forbidden. And every time you did, shame grew just a little bit more, took a little stronger hold, and continued to erode at your life and your connection with others."[2]

Dr. Brene' Brown has studied extensively on the subject of shame and she says that "Shame grows exponentially in environments of secrecy, silence, and judgment." That's profound. In other words, the less we share and speak about and receive empathy and grace for the things that we've said or done or left unsaid or undone that we're ashamed of, the larger the shame grows associated with those actions or inactions, and the more prone we are to continue those behaviors because we are so consumed by the shame and the belief that we are innately bad people because of it. So we begin to consistently act out what we believe.

Sometimes this shame has its origin in our childhood because oftentimes children who are physically, verbally, emotionally, or sexually abused grow up feeling enormous shame. Because the mistreatment was also a misjudgment, it can cause a person to believe that they are not a good person. Therefore, their behaviors are shaped by their self-image that was formed in the construct of abuse.

The most effective remedy and cure for shame is to take the risk of being vulnerable enough to tell our secrets to people who we trust will steward our stories with confidentiality and love. Then we must receive and extend ourselves the grace and mercy that will evaporate our shame.

CHAPTER 4

THE GIFT OF EXPOSURE

In John 7:53—8:11 there is a passage of Scripture that has some controversy with it regarding its canonical legitimacy. If you have a copy of the Bible handy and you turn to this passage, you'll probably notice that there is usually some commentary or note associated with it—something to the effect that the most ancient manuscripts and many other ancient witnesses do not have John 7:53—8:11 in their writings. In fact, some church historians and even Church fathers and biblical commentators will end their research and commentary at John 7:52 and resume their work at John 8:12, omitting this story altogether. The story is about a woman who was allegedly caught in the very act of committing adultery. She was then brought by a group of men to Jesus to be condemned to death, which was the penalty for her sin/crime. And just before the woman was to be executed, Jesus gave a directive to the anxious stone-throwers. He said, "Whoever is without sin in their lives, you cast the first stone."

Now parenthetically, I think it's noteworthy that out of the seven most respected manuscripts from which the sixty-six books of the Bible has been compiled, six of those manuscripts don't include this story; *however, most* of the scholars associated with these manuscripts believe that the story actually did happen. They just don't agree that it should be a part of the Bible. Many of the scholars who omit this from the biblical text or include it with a disclaimer, have come to this conclusion because in their opinion, Jesus' approach to this woman's sin was too soft. Therefore, if people read this as a part of the Bible, they may be inclined to believe that it's *okay* to commit adultery. But that's not what Jesus said at all. In fact, He clearly told the woman not to ever do again what she had been brought to Him for doing. He said to her, "Go and sin no more." But the fear of these Early Church Fathers was that if persons who had been delivered out of sinful pasts, didn't have the severe consequence of death attached to such sexual sins as adultery, then these persons would be more easily tempted to return to the lifestyles that they had been delivered out of. I understand that this is always the risk of grace.

People will always be tempted to abuse grace and say, "Well since I know that God loves me, understands me, and will forgive me, I'm not as worried about the consequences of my sins." My response to that is the purpose of grace is not just unmerited pardon for sins, but the purpose for grace is also an enablement to live righteously and obediently to God's commands as well.

But in spite of the debate over whether or not this story should be in the Bible or not, again, very few doubt whether or not the story actually took place. Now there's a lot that can be said and elaborated on in this particular story, and I certainly will not try to do an exhaustive exposition of this story in this book. For a more comprehensive look at the story I've provided a link here of a Sermon that I gave on it: http://www.zionchurchonline.com/sermon-archive-1/the-blessing-of-being-caught

First and foremost, I want to point out that the woman was actually *caught* in the act of adultery, and I call that the *Gift of Exposure,* because like so many who have failed or fallen and been exposed, it's actually a *blessing* to get caught. If nothing else, getting caught brings a halt to a destructive vice or habit in our lives that we usually have made repeated attempts to end on our own, unsuccessfully. And after weeks, or months, or years, or even decades of hiding and living duplicitously, we are finally brought to a screeching halt by being caught. I've heard from police detectives that one of the ways that they know when they've gotten the right person even without interrogation when they arrest someone, who's been an alleged fugitive, is when they placed the arrested person in a room alone, the person will always fall asleep. That happens because running and hiding was such an exhaustive daily effort that getting caught at least gave them a chance to rest. For the leader who gets caught and exposed after an extended period of private failure, there is a strange mix of emotions, combining relief and fear at the same time. Sometimes a leader will reach out for help when they have fallen and confess their sins. At other times, and probably more often than not, the leader is caught.

Maybe a text message is discovered or a hotel receipt. Sometimes it's a failure to cover their tracks well, and they forgot to erase their Internet site history. Sometimes the leader is unexpectedly spotted somewhere by someone in a compromising situation. Sometimes the leader is actually arrested for driving under the influence of alcohol or pulled over while in possession of a controlled substance. Some leaders are arrested for soliciting a prostitute. Others are caught with their hand in the cookie jar of company or ministry finances, using funds improperly for their own personal aggrandizement. Some leaders are discovered through a threat against their family with a knock on their door from a stranger seeking to collect an enormous gambling debt.

Some leaders are caught with drug paraphernalia found in their car or in their travel bag.

On and on the various exposure lists can grow, but whatever the scenario, the leader got caught, and just like the woman caught in the very act of adultery, getting caught can be one of the greatest blessings in their lives. Now in the story of the woman caught in adultery, the people who caught her meant her harm. The blessing is however, they brought her to Jesus! If you're a leader who's been caught, no matter how bad the consequences of your sin, if getting caught brought you to Jesus, then it was a blessing in disguise. Even if you're a christian leader who is leading a seminary or local church or parachurch organization, living in secret sin keeps you away from intimacy with God. But getting caught brings us back to Him in profound and undeniable ways, which makes getting caught a blessing.

My life had become one of public success and private failure. Our church was growing, and we were poised to move into more and more territory, but there was a serious "gas leak" in our organization that would soon blow up and I'm glad it did. You see, because of the consistent compromise in the key relationships in my life, compromise spread *throughout* my life. I compromised my relationship with God, my relationship with Vicki, my relationship with my children, and my relationship with my pastor. I was a walking contradiction. Because I didn't want *any* of the aforementioned people to stand in the way of my success, I operated without their blessing. In hindsight, that's a dangerous journey, but in the moment I couldn't see the danger. I began to compromise my convictions at church. I said we would operate with margin, but I shattered our margin and our reserves with what I'll call, "Operation Movement." A term that I mentioned earlier in this book that's connected to a theme that I've used at Zion Church to identify us as a "movement and not a monument." And although there's nothing wrong with that thematic approach to our ministry philosophically, it was the way that I went about accomplishing this mission that was reckless.

Again, my private world was out of order and lacked margin, and that bled over into my public world of leadership, which was also without order, discipline, and margin. I was operating without a compass at that time as a leader, primarily governed by my self-centered fleshliness. I felt like an adult letting an unlicensed teenager recklessly drive a car in which I was now a passive passenger, all the while praying for mercy but expecting a crash at any moment.

Post-Exposure (Alone)

When a leader is caught, the light that once lit the stage that they led on and highlighted their strengths is now burning with intensity as it now exposes their failures. Seemingly in a matter of seconds, everything that has taken the leader a lifetime to build all comes crumbling down on them at one time. I share a brief but vivid illustration of this point here https://www.youtube.com/watch?v=H1bzugaQr1I. Now that the leader has been exposed, and they've been stripped of their authority and responsibilities, they now take the lonely road to who knows where. What a lonely road it is. Who wants to be around a leader who has let down the very people that they led? The people on their team are shocked. The people in their family are embarrassed. The people in the industry or community in which they led are talking about them in hair salons, on the telephone, and even on social media. And the "star" that once shined is now fallen into a dark place *alone.*

This is by far the most difficult period of a leader's fall—the time when there's really very few people to talk to. Outside of a lawyer or a pastoral counselor or confidante, the leader is shut up to their own thoughts.

How could I have been so stupid?

Why didn't I stop and repent when I had the chance?

Look at what I've done now.

I will never be what I once was.
I'm done.

The intensity of the loneliness for the leader at this point can only be matched by the depth of the hopelessness that he has as well. Some leaders are so depressed at this point that they contemplate or even commit suicide. Others try to painstakingly put together the pieces of their lives into some sort of salvageable future existence far short of what they originally dreamed. Many times their marriages are at stake, in addition to their financial well-being. They've lost credibility, the trust of their organizations, their privacy, their salaries, their benefits and perks, the respect of their families and friends, their sense of purpose, and on and on and on. The losses begin to pile up like pancakes at an IHOP on a Saturday morning.

Alone with God

Somewhere in the shadows of despair—somewhere from an indescribable abyss—these fallen, broken, hopeless leaders whisper from their souls,

> God . . . I know You're probably fed up with me just like everybody else. But if I've got any grace left on my account, I could sure use it now.

You see the thing that I've discovered in my life of nearly a half of a century—a life full of failures and mistakes I might add—is the fact that no matter how far you've fallen or how low you may be, you're never out of the reach of the love, mercy, grace, and forgiveness of God. In fact, God loved us before we blew it, and He was still loving us while we were blowing it. He certainly doesn't love us any less after everyone else found out that we blew it. Hey, it's not like God found out when everyone else did. He knew what was going on all the time, and He loved us enough to expose us.

Alone with Spiritual Siblings Born for Adversity.

Proverbs 17:17 says, "A friend loves at all times, and a brother is born for adversity." I don't believe that's always a biological sibling that God blesses us with through the worst of times, although I am personally blessed to have that in my life. I believe God will bless us with spiritual siblings, who have been born for such a time as this. These are men and women who we may not have even known prior to our moral collapse, but God placed them in our lives because He knew that we would need their support to make it through these dark and difficult times. These are people who've also fallen. They've also misappropriated funds and charitable donations or have been addicted to alcohol or drugs or who've also been sexually addicted to pornography and or have been unfaithful to their spouses. They've walked through the valley that you're now entering as a leader, and their wisdom, prayers, support, and encouragement are absolutely essential to your survival and recovery.

When I fell, God gave me a recovery team of two therapists who focused on different broken parts of my life. One was a marriage therapist to help me reconnect with Vicki on a level that I had never connected with her before. And one was a personal counselor to help me reconnect with God and myself in a way that I had never experienced before. I was also blessed to have a loving, supportive, and no-nonsense pastor, who walked with me every step of the way, and a support group of other church and business leaders, who've walked in my shoes and have come out stronger on the other side of their failures.

Chapter 5

Recovery Work

When a leader falls, one of their responsibilities is cleaning up the part of their life that was soiled and led to their demise. This cleaning up is called "recovery work." This is more than their just being placed on an administrative leave of absence, getting a slap on the wrist, and then returning to work in 90–120 days. No, there is work that must be done to give the leader and the organization the optimal likelihood that this failure will not be repeated. This will require intense work. In fact, the leader may work harder in recovery than they did while running the organization that they led. This includes reading, journaling, counseling, support groups, accountability, meetings, and more reading and counseling and reading and on and on the work goes.

This work includes not only discovering the various components that led to their failure as a leader, but it is also a journey of self-discovery as well. Who am I? Why am I the way I am? What drives me? What scares me? This work can't be done simply with the motive of returning to the leadership position, the leader must truly want to be healed of the internal dysfunctions that caused them to fall from the wall of leadership.

If the leader's fall was drug- or alcohol related, it could very well mean a significant amount of time in a drug and alcohol rehabilitation facility and program. It will mean regular drug testing, meetings with drug and alcohol counselors, and an allegiance to and commitment to sobriety. It could mean changing their social circles and not frequenting old places and environments that can cause them to relapse into their past addictive behaviors. It will mean reorienting their entire lives to cope with and manage people, life, and problems without using alcohol and or drugs to comfort or medicate them. They will have to learn how to be afraid and worried and anxious and stressed and pressured and experience those feelings without numbing themselves with substance abuse. They will have to live life one day and one hour and one moment at a time, fighting and resisting and avoiding the temptations all around them to get drunk or high again. They are no longer free to drink as they please. That liberty was forfeited when they finally got caught. Now they must live with others in mind—alcohol free.

For the record, I believe in 100 percent sobriety from any addictive behavior that led to a costly demise in a leader's life as a life goal. I believe that it is essential for the leader's long-term success that they not have any level of involvement with the behavior that may have cost them almost everything of value in their life. And the reason why I believe 100 percent sobriety is necessary for any leader who fails is because as the old saying goes, "one drink is not enough, and a thousand is not too many." Indeed, one drink, one marijuana joint, or one cocaine hit can take them right back over the edge into even worst addictive behavior. And 100 percent sobriety and integrity and abstinence also goes for the leader whose failure was around money, gambling, unbridled authority, sex, or any other vice. I like the words of Warren Buffet when he says, "It takes 20 years to build a reputation and 5 minutes to ruin it. If you think about that, you'll do things differently."

RSVPs Back to the Dungeon

One of the realities that every fallen leader who is in the process of recovery must be aware of is the fact that the temptation to go back into whatever had them ensnared before will always linger around the corner. Every fallen leader must realize how close they live to a relapse. The leader will regularly receive what I call unsolicited "RSVP invitations to go back to the dungeon of darkness" that they were blessed and fortunate enough to be rescued out of. The tempter knows your address and mine, and he keeps us on his mailing list, constantly inviting us to another round of pleasure and power. Sometimes these invitations or temptations or solicitations are so strong and enticing that it takes a lot to resist them. And there are a few reasons why these RSVPs occur.

Memory

One of the things that repentance and recovery work doesn't eliminate is our memory. In fact, the more sober we are and the healthier our lives become, the clearer our mind becomes, and the memories of what we once did and how we once conducted ourselves tend to be very clear as well. Sometimes our minds will give us flashbacks. We'll see ourselves in a casino, gambling through the night, and we'll remember all that came with it that was both pleasurable and painful. We'll remember the thrill of victory and the rush that it gave us to feel like we conquered the giant. We'll remember vividly the agony of defeat and the fear and despair we felt, having gambled away our wedding rings and watches because we just couldn't find the power to stop. Because most of our deviant behavior and decisions as leaders is stored away in our long-term memory center of our brains, the data is easily accessible.

We remember the secret meetings with our drug dealer. We remember the secret locations and the efforts to hide and cover our tracks. We remember the rush of the high that we got when the drug took over our minds, and we started floating away mentally beyond all of our problems into a world of peace and pleasure and no problems. We remember our bodies craving the drug and longing for another hit, and the satisfaction that came across our faces when we finally got to our stash and our supplier. Nothing else mattered at that time. No one else mattered at that time. *I just need a hit right now. I just wanna get away.* Then we remember when we came down off of our high, panicking and trying to get ourselves together. We were not sure what actually occurred while we were blindly high and not sure if we were robbed, taken advantage of, photographed, videotaped, or left alone. We remember looking at our watches and wondering what day it was and trying to figure out again how we're going to respond to five missed calls from our spouses and several missed text messages from our children saying, "Daddy, where are you?"

What project at work are we going to blame this time? What story are we going to make up this time? Who can we get to lie for us and be a phony alibi for us this time? So we put Visine in our eyes and reach for our stash of mouthwash and gum for our breath. We keep the windows down in the car as we drive, no matter how cold it is to try to air out any fragrance remnants in our clothing that may reveal where we really were and what we were really doing. We remember all of these things so vividly. And the irony of it is, as reckless and dangerous as those times were, we are still regularly invited to re-engage in them.

Euphoric Recall

The euphoric high felt during drug or alcohol abuse directly affects an area of the brain called the pleasure or reward center. This is the same part of the brain that manages a variety of important psychological functions such as the following:

- Emotional response
- Anxiety management
- Coping with stress
- Reinforcing behaviors (forming habits)
- The ability to resist impulses
- The formation and recollection of memories

Drugs and alcohol provide real, albeit temporary, relief of emotional pain or distress in this part of the brain. When the substance wears off and the underlying psychological disorder begins to take over, the brain will use every psychological tool at its disposal to get those chemicals again. One of the most problematic of these symptoms—especially after months of recovery—is a phenomenon called *euphoric recall.*

How Euphoric Recall Works

Since the formation and recollection of memories is managed in this same area, the brain may choose only to bring to mind the fun times or highlights of past drug use. The user will not remember the pain, sickness, destruction, disappointment, or trapped feelings of addiction—only the good times. This can lead a person to romanticize their previous substance abuse and spend too much time thinking back on it longingly.

How to Stop Euphoric Recall

While you cannot stop euphoric recall, one of the most powerful tools to overcome it is through relational accountability. Make sure you have a friend or sponsor who you have especially empowered to hold you accountable for your time, words, money, and actions. Another person can provide the accurate perspective that euphoric recall destroys. You may start to become nostalgic for your party days, but a good accountability partner will remind you of the broken relationships, the misery of withdrawal, and the positive aspects of being clean and sober. Journaling can also be extremely helpful—especially as it relates to identifying faulty or incomplete memories and filling in those gaps during weak moments. In time you can train your mind to remember all aspects of the disease of addiction, not just the distorted ones.

Two scriptures come to mind when I think of the power of euphoric recall, the first being John 5:14

> Later Jesus found him at the Temple and said to him, "See, you are well again. Stop sinning or something worse may happen to you."

Relapsing

Relapsing is a term used in the world of recovery and addiction treatment work, and it's synonymous with the Christian concept of backsliding. Jesus is basically saying to this man in John 5:14 that He miraculously healed after suffering for thirty-eight years, "Don't get back into what got you shut down for thirty-eight years." By the way, you would think that after suffering for thirty-eight years for anything, that that would be long enough to cure the person of whatever it was that they were hooked on, but it's not always that simple. Some stuff doesn't ever go away—not in this lifetime. Therefore, we may have to fight for our sobriety regarding that thing for the rest of our lives. So Jesus says to this man, "Don't relapse. Don't backslide. Don't you go back out there and do what you did before. Because *this* time around the consequences will be *worse* than they were the last time." Wow!

Then the second verse that comes to mind when I think of euphoric recall is Proverbs 26:11, "As a dog returns to its vomit, so a fool repeats his folly." A dog vomits because it is in some kind of internal pain, and therefore throws up what is bothering it internally. As soon as that pain is gone and the memory of how much pain the thing caused is gone, the dog can only sense the good in what it has just rejected, and wants to partake of it all over again. As humans, no matter how much pain our destructive actions or words or behavior has caused us, once the pain subsides and we can only euphorically recall the pleasure associated with the behavior, we go right back to doing the thing that had us throwing up in pain before.

Gabor Maté is a medical doctor who works in Vancouver Canada with patients with various addictions. He wrote a book entitled, *In the Realm of Hungry Ghosts*. "Hungry ghosts" are mystical creatures in Buddhist teachings that have very narrow and scrawny necks, but *huge, empty stomachs*. The idea behind these creatures is the fact that they can never fully be satisfied because their appetites are greater than their capacity to fill them. Therefore, *nothing outside of them can ever truly fulfill them*. That in many ways is a picture of addiction. A person who is addicted is insatiably hungry and barrenly empty on the inside and yet can only find ways to *temporarily* quell those longings through some form of addictive behavior. But before long the famished feelings return, and the need for another hit arises. *Being addicted means we continue to seek external things to fill or heal internal issues.*

Triggers

Another reason why we get RSVPs back to our old dungeons of darkness is because we experience some kind of emotional pain and disappointment in our lives that we used to medicate with our past destructive choices and behavior. And those "triggers" are powerful because they set in motion a series of reactions that if we're not careful can take us right back down the same patterns that led us to our bondage in the past. For example, we could be months or years down the road in our recovery and doing well and then experience some kind of pain or disappointment or feeling of belittling or rejection in our marriage. Immediately we remember how, when we felt that way in the past, we would reach out to our secret lover and they would always make us feel treasured and special and valued. And so now we're once again facing the exact same feelings that fueled our affair before and the RSVP comes in through an internal message, "Hey, would you like to give so and so a call? You know they will never reject you. They *love* you, and they think the world of you. They would never take you for granted. Go ahead reach out to them and see how they're doing or what they're doing and see if you guys can get together again."

More RSVPs while We Sleep

One of the realities of the climb out of sin and failure to a place of consistent virtue and integrity and trustworthiness as a leader is that you will have a combination of *flashbacks* and *re-invitations* to your past unseemly behavior and choices through dreams. Dreams remain a mystery for the majority of our society, both in religious and secular contexts. Scholars have been baffled for centuries over the meaning and even the purpose of dreams, although there seems to be agreement as to what stage of our sleep they occur. What I have personally discovered through my own experience and through conversations with several leaders who have experienced some sort of moral failure during their leadership tenure, is that there are times, following their repentance and recovery, that they will have very vivid dreams reminding them of the time period that they'd love to forget. People who they drank with or slept with or got high with or gambled with or stole with will often invade their dreams because they were literally a part of their dark past. Dreams can be powerful tools of temptation to lure us back into our old ways of thinking and behaving. But I believe we can utilize those kind of dreams to help to sober us and remind us of the kind of person that we are still capable of being, while continuing to resist the pull to go back to the dungeon that God delivered us out of.

Now these "RSVPs" are really powerful and are the reason that a lot of leaders go into relapses. Whether they are the result of our memories or they're born out of emotional triggers or we experience them through dreams, we have to have a system in place to continually reject and decline those invitations.

Here are a few:

Support Groups

Reach out before you act out, or as the saying goes, "Call before you fall." Whenever you are tempted as a leader to re-engage in former destructive behaviors, it is imperative that you reach out to someone who is committed to your purity and your success and tell them you are being tempted and that you're having a difficult time. Call, text, or send emails. Reach out, not just to one person because they may not be available. Reach out to a group of people who understand what it means to get an RSVP and who can help you survive this temptation storm.

Prayer

Know that God is pro-you. He is on your side and on your recovery team. Praying to Him during, as well as before and after an RSVP, is important. Especially during a time of temptation, we need to pray and ask God to help us to survive. Here's a sample emergency prayer in times like that:

> Dear God, I plead with You to help me right now. I am being tempted to go back into a place that You have graciously pulled me out of. Father, don't let me go back no matter what. Help me to weather this storm without going backward. Make me stronger. Grant me the grace that I need to make it through this time. I prefer peace and purity more than hiding and cheating and lying. I prefer living my life openly, rather than living in fear and anxiety day after day. Lord, help me to see this temptation for the ugly thing that it is: an attempt to utterly ruin my life. In Jesus' Name, amen.

Reflection on Consequences

Sometimes it is helpful to remember how much trouble you were in as a leader because of the very thing that you're being invited to return to. You can even contemplate how much worst things *could've* been for you and how bad things might actually be this time around if you go back to that place that always promised more than it delivered. Remember the guilt, shame, anxiety, stress, fear, and anger and self-loathing that you went through when you were "having such a great time" with your past. These things can be very helpful deterrents to RSVPs when they come your way.

CHAPTER 6

THE RECALL

There are times when automobile manufacturers will do a "recall" on certain makes and models of their vehicles because of some malfunction that was discovered as a result of an accident of some sort. Therefore, to avoid litigation or further harm to customers or the reputation of the company, even if it's 480,000 vehicles affected by the recall, the company will have every one of those vehicles brought in to replace and repair the deficient part of the car for free. This is done so that the people who use the vehicles will be safe, and the company that makes the vehicle will preserve the integrity of its products.

Similarly when God has a leader who has an "accident" or a failure that hurts the people that follow that leader, He will often call that leader away from the leadership platform into His laboratory of discipline and correction to work on the deficiencies that caused that leader to crash. God does this so that the leader won't continue to move about unrepaired and end up hurting more followers. And God does it to protect the integrity of His name and the position the leader is privileged to have. The purpose of the recall is to heal and repair the leader so that the leader can one day return to leadership service, better prepared and equipped to lead. In the Gospels (the first four books of the New Testament), I'm amazed by the fact that after Jesus Christ first called the disciples into service and they began serving Him in their ministry assignments, when Jesus died, and the disciples were overcome with grief and disbelief, Jesus *still* wanted to use these same guys who failed to remain faithful during difficulty. Jesus recalled them and told them to preach the Gospel to every creature (Mark 16:15).

On the Bench and Out of the Game

I personally thought when I had been exposed for my failures as a leader that I was done. I really didn't think that I would ever be allowed to return to ministry leadership and certainly not back to the church that I had been leading. I had let so many people down, and so many people were hurt. So many people lost their jobs. So many people's confidence in me was shattered. So much money was squandered and wasted. I truly believed that my failure was not salvageable. But, ironically, I may have been the only one thinking that way.

My loving and supportive wife never believed that I was done. My loving pastor never believed that I was through and useless. Even my therapists all believed that I had a future in ministry and that my life would actually be better than anything that I had experienced beforehand. All of their support and belief was so very encouraging to me. I now want to encourage you as you read this book. God is not through blessing and using you. Your best days of leadership service are still in front of you. You just have to let him do the work in and on your life that's necessary for you to be prepared for longevity of service.

I remember when there was a time during my journey of recovery that my pastor called me and said on a particular date that I could return part-time to my leadership role. I was so amazed. I felt like a player on a sports team who always sits on the bench, watching the game but never gets in the game under any circumstance and never even expects the coach to call his name when he's looking for a substitute to give rest to one of the regular players. When that bench player's name is called, he looks at his coach with bewilderment and says, "Who, Me?" That's how I felt when my pastor called me to get back in my leadership role. "*Who, Me?*" I thought. Me? Humpty Dumpty? Me? The one who blew a public trust? Me? The one who let down my family, my friends, my church, and my Lord? Are you sure you're referring to *me?*"

I'm still amazed by it and I can truly say that being back in my old leadership role is a blessing that I don't take lightly. Knowing that I don't deserve to be in this place of leadership again makes it all the more precious. What I've experienced from God and tasted in my life through all of this is what I would call a *sweet grace*.

Rahab the Harlot

One of my favorite biblical characters is an Old Testament "working girl" named Rahab. Rahab is famous for her depraved career and for hiding two Israelite spies in her home and literally saving their lives. In fact, her heroism is so celebrated biblically, that she is listed among the greatest spiritual leaders in history, in Hebrews 11 in what some call "Faith's Hall of Fame." There among the likes of Abraham and Moses and David and Jepthah and Gideon and Enoch and many others stands this prostitute who heroically helped the Israelites during a critical time in history. But the irony of her story is the fact that while no other name in that historic list is chronicled along with their sin of choice or record, Rahab's name remains accompanied by what she once was, a harlot. Rahab the Harlot is how she's always mentioned.

David is not called, "David the Adulterer." Abraham is not called, "Abraham the Liar." Moses is not called, "Moses the Murderer." But Rahab is called, "Rahab the Harlot," followed by the great work that she did. Her history (hooker) and her "ministry" (Israelite spy protector) remain in the same sentence. And although I think it's a bit unfair I like it. I like the fact that God has kept her history and her ministry close enough together so that she will never forget what a *privilege* it is to be used by Him.

That's my experience, as well. My failure (history) remains close enough to my ministry service that I am keenly aware that it's only by the grace of God that I'm still in the game. And I say to all of us fallen, broken leaders, who by the grace of God have been allowed to return to leadership: never let your failure get so far away from you that you forget what a privilege it is to be back in the game.

CHAPTER 7

THE REBUILDING

One of my favorite television shows growing up was Lee Major's role as Colonel Steve Austin in the action-packed show *The Six Million Dollar Man.* As the story is fictitiously told, Astronaut Austin is severely injured in an aircraft crash causing him to lose an arm, both legs, and an eye. Miraculously, through the advancement of scientific medicine, both of his legs, his arm, and his eye are all surgically replaced with bionic equipment, giving him superhuman speed, bulldozer strength, and infrared, 20:1, zoom-lens vision capabilities. The cost of the surgical rebuilding of Colonel Austin was $6 million, thus the title of the show. Now as a kid, I was always captivated by the ninety-second intro to the show that was a reenactment of Austin's crash and surgery. I remember vividly the words from Steve just before the crash, when he says, "Flight Com . . . She's breaking up, She's breaking up," as he referenced the condition of the aircraft that he was on.

Following the crash, the narrator comes on and says, "Steve Austin, Astronaut. A man barely alive." Then the voice of what appears to be one of the members of the medical staff attending Colonel Austin comes in, "Gentlemen, we can *rebuild* him . . . We have the technology . . . We have the capability to make the World's first Bionic Man . . . Steve Austin will be that man . . . Better than he was before . . . Better, stronger, faster." Then there's music and video footage of the post-surgery Steve Austin, running at sixty miles per hour—amazing stuff.

That was one of the most powerful television intros that I've ever seen and I believe that it serves as a great analogy to what can happen to leaders who have crashed morally. I believe that each one of us can be rebuilt and we can be better than we were before—better, stronger, and wiser. I also believe that it starts with rebuilding our character.

Rebuilding Character

One of the key ingredients to leadership is *character*. In fact, character is so essential to leadership that it is the lack thereof that causes leadership failure, and it is the rebuilding of character that prepares a leader to steward effectively their second chance. In my opinion, character determines our success and futures more than anything else—even more than networking or talent, because even if you have the connections through favoritism or nepotism to *get* a leadership role, you're still going to need character to *maintain* that role. Indeed even if you're one of the most talented people on the planet in your particular profession, in the words of the late Ed Cole, "Your talent can take you places that your character can't sustain you." So we have to get better in life, not just at what we do professionally, but at who we are as people internally. That is not to minimize the value of competency and connections in the world of business and ministry, but it is intended to maximize the importance of character in the leader's life and work.

You Can't Go Like That

I remember one day when my kids were really small that Vicki and I decided to bless them with a trip to Chuck-E-Cheese. Now for those of you who may be unaware of what Chuck-E-Cheese is, it's a combination Pizza Restaurant and Indoor-Mini-Adventure-Park for kids. And when *my* kids were little, it was a very popular place. On the day when I announced to my kids that we were going to Chuck-E-Cheese, as expected, my kids went crazy with excitement! "Yeah, we're going to Chuck-E-Cheese!" was a chant that I'm sure could be heard by my neighbors! Ironically, I don't even remember my children even speaking to me that day prior to the Chuck-E-Cheese announcement, but following the announcement, I got hugs, and thank you Dads galore.

Of course, I did what every good dad would do at that point; I took advantage of their enthusiasm and used the trip to Chuck-E-Cheese as a negotiation tool and leverage to get work done by my kids. (It works every time.) "As soon as you all clean up all of the toys in the basement," I said, "and clean up your rooms, we can go to Chuck-E-Cheese." When children have that kind of motivation, it makes chores not even seem like work to them. They were singing, dancing, and working all at the same time. "We're going to Chuck-E-Che-ese. To Chuck-E-Che-ese. A C-H-U-H-E-C-C-E-K-C (They were all under six) Chuck-E-Cheese. To Chuck-E-Cheese!!!"

After they pretty much detail cleaned their rooms, and it was time to go, I remember that my precious daughter Asha, (who must have been six at the time) came bouncing down the stairs in an adorable little pink-and-white summer outfit: She had on pink-and-white polka-dot shorts with a matching pink-and-white top. She had pink-and-white barrettes in her hair, and she had the little white girly socks on with the little pink-trimmed fold-down designs around the edges. She looked breathtaking, and she did all of this by herself. She even had on her little pink-and-white tennis shoes that had the little flashing lights on them. The girl reminded me of her fashion-coordinated father—matching from head to toe.

The only problem was, it was *November*, and it was probably about forty degrees outside. So I sent her back upstairs to her room and said, "You are not going out of here in this cold weather like that." And she was *crushed*. The reason why she was crushed was because she didn't cue in on the "like that" portion of my statement; she just assumed she wasn't going to get to go to Chuck-E-Cheese and it *devastated* her. So after a few moments, I went upstairs to check on her and saw her crying, still in her summer wear, and I asked her why she was crying. She said, "Because I wanted to go to Chuck-E-Cheese." And I said to her, "Asha, you *are* going to Chuck-E-Cheese; you're just not going *like that.*"

Now I shared that story (with Asha's permission), to make this point. There are some places that we all want to get to and go to in life. As leaders especially, we all have some things that we want to do and achieve in life. I believe that there are indeed some things and places that our Heavenly Father wants to take us to and get us to but we often don't get there because there's one problem: We can't go the way that we are. It's not necessarily because we have on the wrong attire for the journey; it's not really about *clothes*—it's about *character*.

For me, one example of this was my senior year in high school. I had spent most of that year doing what I had done most of my school life: being a clown, making inappropriate and disrespectful remarks in class toward my teachers and making jokes in class, distracting my fellow classmates, and just being an overall nuisance. It came down to the week before the final week of school for the ninth-to-eleventh graders and the final day of school for seniors, when all of us seniors were supposed to basically meet with all of our teachers and sign out at which point we were finished with high school—done! We could then clean out our lockers, say goodbye to everyone, and not return to school again until our graduation rehearsal. And that's exactly what all of the seniors did in my graduating class. That is everyone, except me. You see, although I guess most of my teachers were glad to see me and my comic show hit the road, there was one teacher who was going to get the last laugh. His name was Mr. Paul Pinsky and he was my Geography teacher.

When I went to each of my other teachers to sign out, they all signed me out and wished me well, but when I got to Mr. Pinsky he said, "Well Keith, I've got some bad news for you . . ." Now you have to understand, that this was the teacher who was once pointing to a Country on a Map in Geography class and asked us students to tell him what country it was. I frantically raised my hand, and he ignored me and called on another student who said the name of a country that was incorrect. Again, while I'm now waving both hands, hoping he would call me, he skipped me again, knowing that my answer would be an intentional attempt to make the class laugh, and called another student, who also gave the name of a country that was incorrect. I think he went through about five or six students before he finally called on me, and I gave him the answer that I was planning to give from the time he first asked the question.

"Keith?" he called.

"Your mother!" I replied. And of course, I got what I wanted, a robust laugh from my fellow students. But I also got what I didn't want, and that was detention. That was just *one* of the many things that I did to annoy Mr. Pinksy during the course of the school year.

I thought it would be good for you to know the history associated between us when he said to me on that supposed last day of school for me,

"Keith, I've got some bad news for you." He went on to say, "Uh . . . you came up a tad bit short . . . You didn't quite pass my class." While I was standing there alone with him dumbfounded and humiliated, he went on to say that he had an extra-credit assignment for me to do if I wanted to pass the class. The assignment was to write a thirty-page paper for him on "Why I Want to Be a Clown" *and,* in addition to that thirty-page paper, I had to read a 538-page small-print book about the Jewish uprising in Warsaw. He also added that he would know if I read the book because he would be asking me specific questions about the book's content. Oh, and I had to get all of that done in a week, or I couldn't graduate.

So there I was, the only senior who had to spend the final week in school with the underclassmen because all of my poor *character* decisions had caught up with me. Now, in order for me to complete the assignment and graduate with my high school class, I basically had to take NoDoz and work and read around the clock for seven days. At a time when I was supposed to be out shopping for my graduation outfit and mailing graduation invitation cards, I couldn't do any of that because I wasn't sure if I would make it. And even though it was actually time for me to move forward with the rest of the seniors in my high school, my *character* held me back.

Indeed, *our character determines our success and future more than anything else.* I believe character is more powerful than faith because you can have faith that can move mountains, but one character flaw that's unchecked and uncorrected can keep you living in a valley, far beneath your vision and dreams. You can even have talents and abilities that are off the chart, and yet your character won't let you reach your full potential. Our character can literally affect how far we can go in life. It has the potential to limit us or launch us.

Maybe you've wondered at times in your own life: "Why am I not where I feel I should be or where I desire to be in life? Is it that I don't have enough talent?" Maybe, maybe not. "Is it my race or gender that's holding me back?" Possibly; but maybe not. But I can tell you one thing for sure that is absolutely guaranteed to hold you back if it's not strong, and that is your character.

What I mean by character is our *moral strength,* our *constitution,* our *attitude, personality,* and *reputation* all rolled together. It is that which determines more than anything else, our success and future. What's holding so many people back in life is not their professional skills; it's their character, their attitudes, and their inability to get along with others. It's getting into fist-fights and altercations at school or even home and using anger-laced profanity towards people through emails and social media. It's not speaking kindly to people or not speaking to people at all at work. Then we scratch our heads, wondering what's holding us back when the reality is no matter how talented a person may be, bad character is almost impossible to overcome when it comes to our success and progress in life.

You can have more experience than someone else, more education, training, and credentials than someone else, and even be smarter than someone else, but if you don't have strong character, it will greatly hinder your progress and success. This is critical for us to grasp and understand because the mistake that far too many of us make is that we continue to look outside of ourselves instead of inside of ourselves for the reasons why we are not where we want to be or feel we ought to be in life. We blame racism, classism, sexism, and every other "ism" we can think of to make excuses for our underachievement in life. We say things like, "They don't like me. I'm the wrong color. I'm the wrong sex. I just keep catching bad breaks. I have bad luck. I married the wrong person. I accepted the wrong job. I was born into the wrong family. I went to the wrong school. And while at the wrong school, I picked the wrong classes and major, and I ended up having the worst teachers." And on and on and on the excuses go.

Here's the problem: it's *never you!* It's *always* someone or something else, and here's the deal: we cannot grow until we realize that *we* are our greatest hindrance for growth.

Character Determines Our Future (Reuben)

In Genesis 49, Jacob, or Israel as he was sometimes called, was about to die. And just before he died, he called his twelve sons by his bedside to speak a final benediction and blessing over each of their lives and the lives of their descendants. This was a very critical moment in each of the lives of those twelve men, and interestingly enough, the blessing that each would receive would be based on their *character.* In fact, Genesis 49:28 summarizes this final scene of Jacob's life by stating, "And all these are the 12 Tribes of Israel (Jacob), and this is what their father said to them when he blessed them, *giving each the blessing appropriate to him.*" (NIV) (emphasis mine). Meaning, the blessings that they received were in proportion to their character. In other words, their characters determined their success and their futures more than anything else. Each son's future was predicated on his character.

No matter how great the son's *potential,* the defining factor regarding his future was his character, regardless of how rich and wealthy their dad Jacob was. Silver spoon or not, the success and future of the sons of Jacob was determined by their character. Now because of the time and space it would take, I won't go through all twelve sons here, but just to drive home the point, let's take a closer look at the first son, Reuben. In verse 3, Jacob says this about Reuben, "Reuben, you are my firstborn, my strength, the child of my vigorous youth. You are first in rank and first in power" (NLT).

Reuben is described as having preferred status in his family among his siblings because of his birth order. He was Jacob's oldest son, the firstborn of his mother Leah, who was one of Jacob's two wives. (Jacob also had a wife named Rachel, Leah's sister, and he also had two concubines, or mistresses, as well.) Reuben, being the oldest of all of Jacob's children, had pre-eminence among his brothers. This would position him, by right, to receive the largest inheritance and the most authority from his father's legacy and estate. But all of his rights and privileges alluded to in verse 3 were forfeited because of his character described in verse 4: "But you are as unruly as a flood, and you will be first no longer . . ." (NLT).

The statement "*Unruly as a flood*" is a reference to his *character.* While the statement, "*you will be first no longer*" is a reference to the limitations that his character placed on his *future* and *success.* You see, in spite of what Reuben should have been and what he was literally born to be, he fell short because he didn't have the integrity to live up to his potential. Many of us as leaders can relate to Reuben. We have great potential but have found ourselves acting unruly and out of control. Some of us are incredibly gifted and talented and may have even been born into a great situation, but we have been undependable, unreliable, and unstable.

When an organization has leaders like that, you never know if they're going to come through for you or not. You don't know if they're going to show up or not. It's a coin toss whether they'll follow through on what they've been asked to do or not. When you're dealing with a person like this, you may have to make contingency plans just in case. Since you never know if they're going to act out on you or not, you always have to have things in place tentatively in case their instability rears its head. So you wisely prepare someone else to fill in for them because they're liable to skip the practice or the rehearsal. You prepare your meeting with the anticipation that they will show up late and unprepared if they show up at all. They're as unruly and unpredictable as a storm or flood.

Sometimes this person's instability is in their *finances*. And if you're married to a person like that you almost have to either take over the finances completely or have a separate bank account just to assure that bills are being paid because you don't know what they're going to do financially from month to month. They may decide to erratically quit their jobs. They may decide to invest significant and needed money in some marketing deal that they found out about from a flyer that was left on their car windshield in a grocery store parking lot. They're unstable. They take a class and drop out before it's over. They choose a major in college and change it eight times before they finally quit college all together. They're in a support group one day, and then they're no longer in the group, and they don't even let the people in the group know that they're no longer in. They are just unpredictable.

It's not about intellect. You can be brilliant and unstable. It's not even about talent and potential. It all comes down to character, our internal stability and fortitude. Character is our moral strength and constitution. In the day in which we live, I believe far more emphasis is placed on becoming better at what we do than becoming better at who we are. So subsequently, we're getting better professionally and organizationally, but we're having more and more relational conflicts, and we have secret, personal vices that are out of control. At the end of the day, what may come back to haunt many of our futures if we're not careful is not our *skills* but our *characters*.

I am personally all too familiar with this reality in my own life for it wasn't my talent that caused me to fail as a leader. It was my atrophying character that caused my failure. Yes I was growing professionally as an executive of a growing mega-church, but I was deteriorating internally as a person. It was just a matter of time before I would fall flat on my face.

Back to Reuben—he was a man who was *born* to succeed but didn't have the internal constitution to do it. The end of verse 4 tells us what he did in particular to blow his future and success: "For you went to bed with my wife; you defiled my marriage couch." What Jacob is referring to here is something that happened back in Genesis 35:22 when Reuben had sexual intercourse with his father's concubine, which in today's domestic structure would be considered his stepmother. So when Jacob described Reuben as being as unruly as a flood, he was referring to Reuben's lack of self-control. Reuben had uncontrolled passions. He was out of control. If Reuben got the urge, he would feed his carnal, sensual desires with *anybody,* even his stepmother.

Takeaways

Back in Chapter 3, I talked about the importance of looking at "films" when it comes to *recovering* from a fall or failure as a leader. But what I'm hoping this book will do is to help prevent some leader from falling at all, as well as help some leader who has already fallen to be resourced enough to avoid a moral failure in their future. Subsequently, one of the resources that's needed is the ability to be *aware of our unique character instabilities.* This is a critical point. We all must be aware of our own unique proclivities towards compromise because we cannot overcome what we overlook. As my dear friend Pastor Jeff Simmons puts it, "You can't fix what you won't face." Since there is something dysfunctional and damaged within all of us, we all need the kind of maturity that seeks to know what it is so that we can improve in those areas. Immaturity on the other hand, either avoids the truth or makes excuses for it.

We *have* to work on our characters so that we can do and accomplish everything we were meant to do in our lives. And because life is constantly writing "character checks" against us in the form of tests, trials, and temptations, we need enough character in our accounts to cover those checks. Therefore, I have a little prayer that I pray that's really simple but profound. I invite you on a journey with me in praying this prayer because this prayer is intended to lead us to the insights that we need to become better people. My prayer is simply, "*Lord, show me, me.*" By this I mean, Lord help me to focus on my own character and the ways that I need to grow and improve. "Lord, show me, me."

This prayer is critical, because we tend to be better with a lens than we are with a mirror. By that I mean, we are great at examining the flaws of others but often are ignorant of our own flaws and deficiencies. Therefore, whenever we are tempted to judge or be critical of someone else, we need to stop and say to God in prayer, "Lord, show me, me." Lord, what do

I need to work on in *my* life? Whenever we're about to look down on someone who is struggling with an addiction or a dysfunction of some sort and we're tempted to judge them, instead say, "Lord, show me, me." What do *I* need fixed or corrected in my life? One of the things that you'll discover when you do this important exercise is how *natural* it is for us to inwardly judge and criticize others.

Whether it's a politician, an athlete, a cashier, another driver on the road, or whoever, we are capable of being ruthlessly judgmental, often without words. This may make us experts on evaluating the flaws and idiosyncrasies of others, but being an expert on someone else's flaws won't help me to see what I need to see about me that will make me a better person and prevent me as a leader especially from hurting a lot of people.

CHAPTER 8

CHARACTER AND THE HUMAN BODY

Proverbs 4:20–27 is the conclusion of a conversation that a father is having with his son, in which he is giving his son advice. It is the last of three conversations that he has with his son in this fourth chapter of Proverbs. The first conversation is in verses 1–9 where the father's emphasis to his son is regarding *wisdom.* There he pleads with his son to get wisdom, love wisdom, cherish wisdom, and even exalt wisdom as he shares with his son the benefits of wisdom. Then in verses 10–19, the Father's emphasis to his son is on *staying away from the wicked,* as he shares with his son about the schemes and the dangers of the wicked and the benefits and blessings of staying away from their path or lifestyle. Then we come to the conversation that the father has with his son in verses 20–27 that we'll spend some time examining in this and the next 4 chapters of this book.

In verses 20–27 the father counsels his son regarding the son's character by pointing out the need to be in control anatomically in a way that positively impacts his character. Indeed, this father warns his son about his mouth, his eyes, his heart, and his feet as each body part is vitally important to his character. Let's look briefly at each one of these character lessons from this father and see how they might help us to strengthen our internal constitution so that we can avoid moral failure in the future. What I'd like you to notice first is what the father says to the son at the beginning of each of these conversations. In verses 1, 10, and 20, the father tells his son to *listen* to him.

It All Starts with the Ears

My child, pay attention to what I say. Listen carefully to my words. Don't lose sight of them. Let them penetrate deep into your heart. For they bring life to those who find them, and healing to their whole body. **Proverbs 4:20–22**

The March 15, 1911, edition of the *New York Times* had an article about a church in Manhattan, New York that was physically falling apart. The church was the St. Peter's Roman Catholic Church located on Barclay Street in Manhattan. It was a church that had been standing for seventy-three years without a single crack appearing in its granite walls; and all of a sudden, following the building of a skyscraper right beside it, cracks started showing up everywhere. Apparently the stresses beneath the church's foundation changed once the skyscraper was built, and the church began showing signs of structural distress in several places throughout the building, so much so that it was declared unsafe by the City of New York's Building Department after numerous inspections. Those inspections discovered cracked walls in the building that were over an inch wide and ran for six to ten feet across the church's west wall. Some of the cracks ran all the way up to the roof of the building.

Now understand, we're not talking about *hairline* cracks, we're talking about cracks that are over an inch wide and that run for up to ten feet in length. That's *major* damage. In addition to the cracks, the church structure had begun to bulge near the building's southwest corner. And we're not talking a few inches of bulging, no the bulging was measured in some areas at up to *six feet* in diameter. It was absolutely astonishing! In fact, one of the transoms was cracked above one of the entrance doors, and there were even window ledges on the building made of heavy rock that were actually sagging. The building was literally crumbling. A building that stood for seventy-three years without a single crack in it was now falling apart.

Now here's the amazing discovery and findings of the Building Department inspectors. Not only was the presence of a huge edifice next door causing enormous stress on the foundation on which the church was built, but you're not going to believe this—the Building Department inspectors discovered that the historic St. Peter's Roman Catholic Church had been built on a foundation of sand. Can you believe that? Sand. In fact, when the skyscraper was built right next to the church, it was reported that immense quantities of sand had to be removed before the construction of the skyscraper was begun. So here you have this beautiful church that's caving in, and you can look here to see its beautiful pictures today -- http://www.google.com/search?q=Pictures+of+the+St. Peter's+Roman+Catholic+Church+in+Manhattan,+NYandclient=s afariandrls=enandtbm=ischandtbo=uandsource=univandsa=Xandei =uVd5U-j1LoXisASoh4Ioandved=0CCcQsAQandbiw=1279andbih =6forty-four

This beautiful Church was originally built on something weak; however, the weakness of its foundation was never exposed until something big came into close proximity to it. When that happened, the church building didn't have a strong enough foundation to hold up. It started crumbling. Although the signs of the building's distress, the cracks, the bulges, and the sagging were *visible*, the *cause* of all of the distress was *invisible* because the cause was in the foundation. The only way to stop the crumbling and the bulging and the sagging and the cracks would be to reinforce the foundation.

I share that story because the truth is, we *all* as individuals have a *"building"* that we have built, and that building is called our character. It is our internal fortitude; our constitution. It's literally the stuff that we're made of. All of us have a *foundation* upon which all of our characters have been built. I believe that the foundation upon which all of our characters are built are the *words that we live by*.

How This Works

The words that we live by are basically our life's theme, or motto, or philosophy. We all have certain catch phrases, beliefs, and statements that we have heard and repeated over and over again that literally dictate and influence the way we live and lead our lives. It is those statements that we build our lives and character on. Therefore, they cannot afford to be "sand-like." We have collected these statements, or words to live by, throughout the course of our lives. We've gathered them from home, in school, at the barber shop, in the beauty salon, at church, or on television, the radio, or on social media. They include statements and words like:

- Stay in School.
- Education is the Key.
- Knowledge is Power.
- Family comes first.
- Divorce is not an option.
- Have it your way.
- Live and let live.
- To each his own.
- Look out for number one.
- To thine own self be true.
- You only go around once in life, so grab all of the gusto that you can.
- Y.O.L.O.—You only live once.
- Wise men still seek Him
- Prayer changes things
- Let go and let God.

Those statements and so many more are for many of us the very *bedrock* upon which we build our lives. Besides those statements, there are the more internal statements that we repeat over and over to ourselves that may even have more dominance and control over our lives and characters than any other statement. They may include words like:

- I'm not smart.
- I'm fat.
- I'm ugly or unattractive.
- I wish I had never _____ "
- I'm better than him, her, or them.
- I'm buffed or beautiful.
- I don't deserve this
- Life is not fair.

The truth is there are so many of these phrases and statements, that we could easily fill up the rest of this chapter with all of the many words or sayings that become the very foundation upon which we build our characters. Here's basically how it works, and it's really simple: we hear something

66

said or an opinion given, and particularly if it comes from a source that we respect or look up to; then whatever was said has a greater potential of becoming something that we *believe in* and make our own personal motto. So we'll repeat the statement either internally or audibly or both from time to time in our lives. That means it's now probably at the point where we have not only heard it, but we've now more than likely *owned* it, and that's really the point at which it has an impact on our character.

Now it has a voice in our decision-making, and in what we value, and in many of the choices we make that affect the way that we live. Something as simple as a *few words* that we *heard* have now become words that we govern our lives by and build our character on. This happens to all of us. And so the principle is *our character is built upon the foundation of what we hear and own*. It is not *just* what we *hear*, but the things we hear and *own* or embrace to the point that what we heard becomes a part of our own personal life philosophy.

The reason why this is so critically important to know and understand is because just like the St. Peter's Roman Catholic Church's building in 1911, if our foundation is not solid and correct, then we're building a character that won't stand—especially when something *big* comes into our lives. The only way you can go through life successfully without a solid foundation to build your character on is if your life is totally free of challenges from start to finish. And that, friends, is a fantasy that will not come true. In fact, some of you who are reading this book may be experiencing tremendous challenges in your lives right now like a skyscraper financial predicament that's moved in close, or maybe you're facing a high-rise marital situation that's right in your living room. Perhaps you're facing a very tall medical condition or a huge dilemma at school, work, or in some other relationship. The reality is, whatever our character is built upon is what's governing the way in which you and I process and conduct ourselves during those times in our lives.

If we never realize that our character is affected and shaped by and built upon the foundation of what we hear and ultimately own, then we won't be nearly as careful about the kind of statements and clichés and coined phrases that we hear, repeat, memorize, and embrace. If my whole life and future is hinging on the level of character that I have (because our characters determine our success and futures more than anything else) and if my character is *built* and standing on the foundation of what I hear and own, then I can't afford to take lightly and not pay attention to the words that I'm living by. What if I'm building my entire life, family, career, relationships, and even my faith on *lies?*

In Proverbs 4:20–22 we clearly see how this principle that *what we hear and own is the foundation upon which we build our character.* Verse 20 says, "My son, give attention to my *words;* incline your *ear* to my *sayings."* (Emphasis added). Now the ear is obviously for hearing. That's really the primary purpose they serve us, however, the ears also provide balance to the body. In fact, whenever someone has an ear infection, one of the symptoms is a loss of balance. Even people who have vertigo-type dizziness are treated in their ears. Therefore, metaphorically speaking, our lives could be spinning, spiraling, and out of balance because of the things that we're hearing that are 'controlling our ears'. Now even though the primary purpose of the ears is for hearing, having ears does not make hearing automatic. Throughout the Bible for example, there are a plethora of admonitions to people *with ears* to make sure that they *hear* because the fact is that there are times when people choose not to hear because they don't want to hear what's being communicated. Then there are times, as well, when people with ears are still unable to hear. Sometimes it's due to their health, their focus, their circumstances, or even their maturity. So there are scriptures throughout the Bible that say things like, "And they having ears but do not hear." And verses like, "He who has ears to hear, let him hear," which again serve as a reminder that just because we have ears doesn't mean that we always hear.

In the twenty-first century in which we live, *listening* is not a skill that we are trained to develop. Nowhere in the educational system is this vital skill nurtured. We are taught to read and write and even speak in a comprehensive way. There are courses on reading, writing, and speaking at every academic level of learning all the way through graduate school. There are even seminars, workshops, and conferences that we can attend to sharpen our reading, writing, or speaking skills. But there is no major course of study on the subject of listening. In fact, I've never even heard of *one single class* offered at any level of school on the subject of listening, and yet not being able to listen has caused great trouble for a lot of people.

Now as this father continues to counsel his son, he goes on in verse 21 to say, "Do not let them (my words) out of your sight, keep them (my words) within your heart" (parenthetical explanations mine). So the father tells his son to *take the words that you hear me say, and not only don't let them out of your sight, but store them in your heart.* Wow! Keep your eyes on what I tell you, and cherish it in your heart. Don't just hear what I'm saying but hone in on what you hear me saying by not letting what you hear depart from your eyes. In other words, keep what I tell you in front of you. And in addition to *hearing* what I say, and *honing in* on what I say, the father tells him to *hide* what I say, by keeping his instructions in his heart.

Now by keeping his father's words in his heart doesn't mean that they are to only be a matter of private, inward thought that have no effect on the son's life as if they're some kind of top secret dogma that only an elite group has the privilege to know. No, the idea of keeping these sayings *in the heart* simply means to *memorize* them so that your *life* flows from them. What the father is actually telling his son to do is not just hear what he's teaching him but to *own* it. Why is this so important? Because what we *hear and own is the foundation upon which our character is built.*

When we hear someone's words or sayings and we give attention to it, inclining our ear to it and keeping it before us and in our hearts by repeating it and memorizing it, we are actually hearing it and owning it. Whenever we hear and *own* something, it now has a *voice* in our lives and in our perspectives, values, decisions, and ultimately in our character.

Then the father goes on in verse twenty-two to say to his son, "for they are life to those who find them and health to a man's whole body." Here's what the father is saying: When you hear, hone in on, and hide my words in your heart and own it for yourself, *those words will become your very way of life.* The father is saying to the son, "Son, my words, my sayings, my advice, and my instructions are *life* to those who find them and *health* to their entire body. In other words, what I'm giving you is good for your entire body and soul." What we hear and own is foundational to our very character because our character and lives are developed and protected, not just by keeping bad things out of it, although that's important, but it's also maintained and protected by putting good things in and keeping them there.

Notice that the father doesn't tell his son to make sure he's not listening to the wrong stuff but to make sure that what he's hearing and *owning* is the right stuff because everything you *hear* you don't have to *own or embrace.* This is critical! For far too often, we try to build our character and live as morally upright people by *avoiding* what we consider negative or immoral things. So we try not to do this, and we try not to say that, and we try hard not to go there, and we try hard not to think that. We go out of our way not to look at or listen to this. Although those efforts are admirable, the advice here that was given directly to this son by his father, and indirectly to us by God, is the key to living a life that has developing and strong character is not focusing on what to avoid but on what to consume, collect, and hold on to.

Think about the truth of that statement as it's given in another biblical passage in Psalm 1:1–3, starting with verse 1: "Blessed is the man that does not walk in the counsel of the ungodly, or stand in the way of sinners, or sit in the seat of the scornful." Now that's all about avoiding the negative in life and that *is* important, but I believe the reason why the blessed person described here doesn't walk in the counsel of the ungodly, and doesn't stand in the way of sinners, and doesn't sit in the seat of the scornful in verse 1 is because of what he/she invests their time doing in verse 2–3:

> "His delight is in the Law of the Lord and in His Law does
> he meditate day and night. He is like a tree planted by the
> rivers of water that brings forth its fruit in season and its
> leaf does not wither and whatever he does will prosper."

This person is not just marked by what they avoid but by what they spend *the majority of their time* (day and night) *embracing*. They didn't just avoid junk; they had a steady diet of and were full of good stuff. This first instruction that the father gives his son is critical and foundational to everything else, and it starts with attentive listening and owning the right stuff to lay the foundation on which our character is built. And if we're going to maximize the blessing of the grace that God has for the broken and take full advantage of the second chances that He gives us, we must make sure that we are properly building or rebuilding our characters for today and for the days ahead, so that we're built to last.

What Now?

In light of the principal that what we hear and own shapes our character, it would be helpful to begin to pray for insight and ask God to reveal to us what things we have heard and owned in our lives that may have indeed shaped our character. One of the hints is to pay attention to the things that you say to yourself. In other words, make sure you eavesdrop in on your own self-talk and begin to prayerfully examine the statements that continue to be repeated in your head and in your heart. Then ask yourself and God this question: Should I *continue* to build my life on that statement or belief? This introspection is very important, because it raises our awareness of the kinds of mantras that we are often unconsciously living by. So as you notice yourself talking to yourself or thinking to yourself, at that moment, eavesdrop in on your internal conversation. Whatever you hear yourself saying or thinking, if it's something that you have been thinking repeatedly, it probably in some way has helped to shape your character because the *frequency* with which we hear or reflect on something causes it to affect our belief system.

There's a statement in the Bible that says, "Faith comes by hearing . . ." In other words, whatever we hear a lot has a powerful tendency of affecting our belief and faith. The frequency of a message helps to make it credible because what we hear *often* can shape our faith, our view of ourselves, and ultimately our lives. *Whatever* we are hearing, good or bad, whether it's from external voices or from our own internal voice, if we hear it often enough, will have a powerful impact on our lives and our character. So once we identify the statements that we are regularly reciting and therefore entertaining, then we need to ask ourselves and God this question, "Should I continue to build my life on that statement? Am I on the right track with this statement, or am I doing myself and maybe even others a disservice by holding on to this philosophy/belief? This is a critically important evaluative question because we are all living by some philosophy whether we are always conscious of it or not.

What we hear and own is the foundation on which our character is built, and the best way of discovering what we are standing on in our lives is to pay attention to the statements that we continue to hear and own. And whenever we discover that we've been building our lives on faulty and unhealthy statements, we need to begin the process of abandoning those negative beliefs, replacing them with positive ones. In order to build the right foundation for our character some of our inner thinking and conversations may need to be amended.

Remember St. Peter's Roman Catholic Church? The edifice that was falling apart because it was built on an unstable foundation? Well, what if there are character cracks in our lives that have their roots in a faulty foundation? The only way to correct the cracks is to reinforce the foundation. We do that by replacing some unhealthy statements with healthy ones. Here's my prayer for us:

> Lord, help us to pay attention to our thoughts, our philosophies, and our core beliefs, the very words and sayings that we live and govern our lives by. Please reveal to us not only what those statements are, but whether or not they should continue to guide our lives. If not, help us to replace the wrong words with the right words. In Jesus' Name, amen.

CHAPTER 9

A HEART MONITOR

"Guard your heart above all else, for it determines the course of your life" **Proverbs 4:23.**

There's a park in the Silver Spring area of Maryland that for years, I used as what I would call my *"prayer ground."* It's a place that I would go when I needed to really connect with God and get direction from Him. It's not because I can't have a conversation with God *anywhere,* it's just that for me, that place seemed to awaken me spiritually. It was my prayer ground. And I remember being on one of my prayer walks there once, and for some reason my heart was heavy. I can't remember specifically why my heart was heavy, but I do remember clearly what I learned that day. As I was walking and asking God to lift the heaviness of my heart and lighten my emotional load, I began to sing praise and worship songs to God from my heart. I just intentionally took my attention off of whatever was bothering me and focused on God.

And as I sang to Him about His love and His faithfulness and His mercy, I remember my heart feeling lighter and I began to weep over the goodness of God. I remember that day that as my heart began to lift out of that valley of depression and heaviness that something interesting happened. My heart was lifted through that time of prayer and praise and worship, but then I realized that I also needed my heart to be *healed* as well. That was the epiphany for me. It was as though my burden had been lifted, and I felt so much lighter, but it seemed as though God just made me cognizant of the fact that my heart was still in a vulnerable condition. So I prayed and asked Him to heal the very heart that He had just lifted.

I discovered in that moment that there is a pattern that happens to us as human beings on a heart level. And it goes like this: before we experience a heavy heart, something usually happens to us or in our lives that causes our hearts to be hurt. When this happens, if we don't get God's loving intervention to heal our heavy, "broken" hearts, then we could find ourselves living with a *hard* heart. So, a hurt heart can lead to a heavy heart, which can lead to a hard heart. The signs of a heavy heart are sadness and depression, while the signs of a hard heart are coldness and indifference. It's important to realize however, that the hard heart *started* with a hurt or broken heart. Just like a protective cast is placed upon a broken limb on our bodies to stabilize and protect the injured area, we place an invisible cast on our hearts to stabilize it and prevent further injury.

Although it may be natural for some of us to judge people who have hard hearts because they come across cold and indifferent, the reality is their hearts became that way through a process of hurt and heaviness that went unhealed. The truth is, nobody really wants to have a hard heart, but our hearts sometimes reach that condition because we've carried a heavy, hurt heart that was too painful to bear. So we put this protective cast of distrust and cynicism and anger over our hearts to stabilize it and protect it from further injury. The problem is, regardless as to who or what caused our hearts to be hurt, many times innocent people end up paying for it because you can't just remove your cast when you're with someone that's emotionally safe and put it back on when you're around someone that's emotionally dangerous. It's not that simple; therefore, there are times when people, who don't even pose a threat to us, feel and experience our hard, yet wounded and guarded hearts.

Here's the character lesson in all of this. When I went to the park that day, the condition of my heart was heavy because it was hurt, but thankfully, when I left the park, the condition of my heart was healed, light, and tender. Part of the reason why that happened is because some of the *content* of my heart was good. The songs of praise and worship that were in my heart and on my internal hard drive if you will, helped to literally lift and heal my heart. I learned that not only is my susceptibility to an injured or hurt heart connected to my character but also my ability to recover well from a hurt heart is directly connected to my character as well. Therefore the condition and content of my heart, *reveals* my character. A key part of our bodies that impacts our character is not just our *ears,* as we looked at in the previous chapter, but also our *hearts.*

As someone once said, "The heart of the matter is the matter of the heart," and in my opinion, the *condition* and the *content* of our hearts *reveal* our character. Now what I mean by the *condition* of our hearts is whether or not our hearts are in a state of hurt, heaviness, hardness, or in a state where it's healthy, whole, healed, light, and tender. That's all representative of our heart's *condition.*

And what I mean by the *content* of our heart is what is *engraved* on our hearts? What's *written* on our hearts? What's *stored* there on our internal hard drives, particularly those words to live by that we talked about in chapter 8? The *condition* of our hearts *coupled with* the *content* of our hearts is a revelation of our character. That's true for all of us.

How This Works

Our character is our constitution. It's our moral strength. It's our internal fortitude. Whatever is in our heart, content-wise, and the condition that my heart is in, *reveals* what level and quality of character I have. Before we drill down into that concept, I want to make clear what I mean when I talk about our *"hearts,"* so that we're on the same page. When we speak of our hearts from a human anatomy standpoint, the heart literally serves as a fountain of life to the whole body. Its job is to pump needed blood throughout the body, which is what keeps each part of the body alive. Indeed because of it's critical role, the health of every vital organ even down to the extremities of our bodies depends upon the wellness, strength, and proper function of our hearts. If our hearts become feeble or diseased, our entire bodies will ultimately suffer, which could ultimately lead to our demise and death. That's how the heart functions anatomically.

Metaphorically speaking, our hearts represent our affections, or desires, or the very seat of our emotions and passions, and just as the heart in the natural realm affects the vigor and vitality of our bodies, in the moral realm the heart affects our choices and decisions and ultimately our character. In other words, it is *the organ* that controls the very direction that a life will take. That is why the condition and content of our hearts has such a huge impact on our character. Now remember, it is our character that determines our future and success more than anything else. It is also our character that controls the level of contentment and joy that we have in our lives. In order for us to clearly see what our character really is, we must look into our hearts to experience that discovery.

This is a critical exercise, given our human proclivity towards continuously looking outside of ourselves to others and ideal circumstances to provide our contentment and joy. We are perpetually depending on people and things to fill us and fulfill us, and therefore our lives are continually controlled by how well people treat us and by how well things are going. The truth is, our heart and its condition and content is really where our focus needs to be instead of on circumstances and people because it is in the condition and content of our hearts where the answers to our contentment in life lie. So, how is this done? Well, it takes some work, but one of the ways of getting to what I'll call "the heart of the matter" in our lives is by asking *heart-level, character-probing questions.*

If you're a person who finds yourself on an unenviable ride on life's emotional roller-coaster without knowing how to really get a grip on yourself while going through drama-filled loops and turns and twists in your life because people and circumstances control your feelings, then you have to begin to ask yourself heart-level questions like, "Why does this make me happy or sad?" Or, "What is it about the condition and content of my heart and ultimately my character that's really controlling the way I feel?" If you're a parent, it is helpful to ask yourself questions like, "Why does my child's report card really dominate my thoughts and feelings? What is really causing me to be proud or ashamed or angry?" If those kind of heart-level probing questions aren't answered, we miss out on the opportunity to have some personal character disclosures because we only focused on our child's academic performance and not on what's really going on inside of us.

If you're single for example, and you don't search your heart and say, "*Why do I really, honestly* want to be married? Really? And is my reasoning for wanting to be married fair to the person that I may end up marrying? Would that honor them?" If those kind of character-probing, heart-level questions aren't asked and honestly answered, then you may find yourself in an unhappy marriage that was doomed from the start because of the initial motivation for the marriage relationship. Who knows, after you truly search your heart regarding your true motivation for wanting to be married, you may discover that you really are primarily looking for someone with a steady income to help you with your bills. And if that's the case, you may be just as happy with a non-intimate housemate than you would be with a spouse.

If you're in an unhappy marriage, and you don't check the condition and content of your heart by asking, "What is it about *me* that makes me unhappy in my marriage?" then you will always blame your spouse for your unhappiness.

If you're in a difficult, uncertain, and unstable financial situation right now that's so complex that you not only don't know where you're going to live and how you're going to make it, you're not even sure what you're going to eat today. Yes, even in that situation if you ignore the content and condition of your heart and you don't ask yourself the question, "What am I most afraid of and fearful of during this time and why? And what am I willing to do and what am I not willing to do in this situation and why?" If those kinds of character-probing questions are not asked and you just hustle and bustle and scratch and scrape your way through that situation without pausing to do some heart-level evaluating, then you miss the opportunity to have a self-revelation of who you are and where you are character-wise at that stage in your life.

Now this whole concept and principle that the condition and content of our heart reveals our character is not original at all. In fact, it's the next lesson that we glean by listening in on the advice-laden conversation that the father was having with his son in Proverbs 4. It's obvious to me that the condition and content of his son's heart was vitally important to this father. Let's listen in: "*Above all else, guard your heart, for it is the well spring of life*" (Proverbs 4:23 NIV). The father tells his son that more than you need to pay attention to any other body part in the development of your character, "above all else," this is *the one* that you must give supreme attention to. Guard this area with all diligence.

The Hebrew word translated "guard" in the NIV is a word that has several connotations to it. On the one hand, it means to *keep* in the sense of *maintaining* something or holding someone in custody as if to restrain them as a prisoner. It means holding on to something or someone without relinquishing it. Keep it. But on the other hand, the word also means to *guard* as if to *protect* from an outside enemy or force. Both meanings are intimated in this verse, but the primary meaning should be determined by the context of the verse. And in this context the father has just told his son in verse 21 to *keep* his words and sayings or advice *in the midst of his heart.* And so the same idea of *keeping* is more than likely intended here in verse 23, meaning, guard your heart by holding captive the good things that you have heard with your ears and kept before your eyes in verses 20–21.

It's the idea of protecting a treasure or keeping something important. The way that is done is by storing it in our internal hard drives, or memory banks. So when it comes to keeping or guarding our hearts, it's not just about keeping the bad out but it's about keeping the good in. One practical way that I recommend doing that is by reading a chapter of the Book of Proverbs every day. Just read the Proverbs chapter that corresponds with that day of the month, and whatever jumps out at you in the chapter, lock in on it and continue reciting it over and over again in your mind throughout the day. What reciting it does is guards our heart and character by keeping something good in it. It's putting good *content* on our hearts. We don't do this so that we can flaunt our biblical knowledge; we do it so that when a circumstance comes up in life that challenges us, we are prepared to face it from a position of personal character that has been strengthened by a principle that has been kept or guarded in our hearts.

We can't just *memorize* the principle; we must *utilize* it in real-life situations, which is really what the father is getting at here in his advice to his son because he actually tells his son the reason why it is so important that above all else and with all diligence that he keeps his heart—from it springs the issues of life! So the *heart* is here pictured as a water source from which life surges. It's a wellspring. The analogy would be very clear to the people of that time because they understood that whenever an individual was in charge of a well of water, their job and responsibility was to keep it covered and secured (i.e., kept and guarded) against the entrance of anything that might poison or defile it.

This was vital because the safe keeping of the well was critical to the health and wellness of not only the well keeper, but to his/her family, and it was also important for the wellness of the other members of their community who benefited from the well. The purity of the well determined the quality of what came out of it. And so it is with our hearts. What's surging or coming forth out of our lives is an indication of the *condition* and *content* of our spring or heart. Everything springs from the heart, good or bad. The father is pleading with his son to pay special attention to his heart because everything springs out of it. With all of the time that we spend in our society focusing on our external presentation and appearance, we need to invest time focusing on the condition and content of our hearts.

We're so externally conscious that we'll get plastic surgery, wear hair pieces, and invests thousands of dollars into our wardrobes because we care about how we appear. Meanwhile, with all of the time, money, and attention that we invest in our outward appearance, the thing that's really controlling our lives and relationships and success and future is the condition and content of our hearts.

What Now?

My prayer is that we would ask God to help us to be better with a mirror than we are with a lens. In other words, let's focus more on ourselves, than we do on others. And specifically, may God show us our hearts, both its condition and its content.

> Lord, is my heart healed and whole? Is it light and tender, or is it hurt or heavy or hard? If so, melt my heart with Your love, lift it by Your grace, and heal it with Your merciful touch, please, Lord. Furthermore, Lord, show me the *content* of my heart. What has been engraved on my heart that comes out in my life? What messages, phrases, quotes, words to live by are housed there?

This is very important because the susceptibility to our hearts getting injured in the first place is hinging on the condition and content of our hearts. Moreover, our ability to *recover* from a wounded heart is contingent on those two factors as well. This prayer exercise as well as the daily Proverb exercise are character-developing exercises that are very important because life and relationships as well as circumstances tend to get difficult from time to time, and if we're not maturing and growing in our character, then our capacity to face those difficulties successfully won't measure up.

I'll close this chapter with this analogy. Imagine that I have a small cocktail umbrella (those cute things placed on the top of cocktails for decorative purposes). I also have a huge, over-sized, golf umbrella that is large enough to cover multiple people in the rain. Now although the cocktail umbrella is cute, it's a huge problem when I'm in a storm because with something that small, even a drizzle will cause me to get wet. Sometimes we've worked so hard on being "cute" but have left our storm-bearing character dwarfed and underdeveloped. As storms and winds and rains and even temptations are sure to come in our lives, sometimes with great ferocity, we are left with a shallow covering or character to handle some deep troubles in our lives.

But the bigger umbrella provides me the preparation that I need before the storm and the protection that I need in the storm, and although a big umbrella won't stop a storm, it will certainly better equip me to get through one. In fact, a light rain, leaves me un-phased when I have a huge umbrella, but if I've got a cocktail umbrella, a light rain will leave me soaked. The point is, when our characters are small and immature, even small things become huge problems. But here's the good news. We can all grow the size and capacities of our characters. As we ask God to help us see what we need to see in our hearts and help us to deposit or replace what we need to, we will begin growing our heart muscle in an amazing way. And although we won't be problem free, we'll be so much better prepared to handle them.

So, may we prepare ourselves for a spiritual open heart surgery, so that whatever bad things are causing us to experience blockage can be opened up, and whatever new content we need to make our spring flow more powerfully and purely can be deposited into our hearts. And may we have clean hearts. I pray in Jesus' name, amen.

CHAPTER 10

WATCH YOUR MOUTH

*"Put away from you a deceitful mouth, and perverse lips far from you" **Proverbs 4:24.***

S everal years ago, about twenty-five people from my staff along with some key volunteers took a road trip from Maryland to Atlanta, Georgia to spend a week of observation and training in how to do church ministry in a more effective and comprehensive way, and in my opinion, the trip had a positive impact on our church. However, something happened on the trip that I'm not proud of at all, and I'm going to spend a little time in "the confession booth," sharing with you what happened. On our final night there in the Atlanta area, our group had a private dinner together in our hotel, and it was a powerful night of sharing and testimonies as we all recapped our experience and the impact that this trip and training had on us. And when it was my turn to share, I shared what the trip meant to me as well, but for some reason, on that night, I was feeling a bit naughty and at the time that I was sharing, I asked the group if I could do a comedy routine with them. Now I can't tell you why I wanted to tell jokes at that point; maybe it was because I had spent the entire week focused hard on learning and taking notes and applying lessons learned, and maybe I just felt the need for some comic relief. I don't know. But nonetheless, I put the request out there before our group to do an extemporaneous stand-up comedy routine.

Now let me give you a little background about me that many of you reading this book may not know. I was *born* into a family of jokesters. Both of my biological parents (who are divorced) as well as my brother are some of the craziest, funniest people you'll ever meet. And for us, making jokes, playing the dozens, making fun of people or situations, and just making people laugh in general is just what we naturally do—all of us. It's not like there's *one clown* in my biological family that sort-of stands out as the odd one in the bunch, and the rest of us are normal. No, in my family, it's four for four. Every single one of us are literally unpaid comedians. Which, by the way, is why I can't understand why I would get in so much trouble at home when I would get in trouble at school for being a clown. I mean it's not like I wasn't genetically disposed to that kind of foolery. What do you expect?

Anyway, when I was a kid, I dreamed of what I would be when I grew up, just like all of my other friends, but unlike many of them, I really didn't dream of being a police officer or firefighter or attorney or doctor or any of those honorable professions. I had one real ambition as a kid—I wanted to be a stand-up comedian, period. I was funny, I made people laugh, and I wanted to make a living doing it. Period, end of story, that's it. My heroes growing up outside of a few professional athletes, were Richard Pryor, John Belushi, George Carlin, Laurel and Hardy, Abbott and Costello, the Three Stooges, Redd Foxx, and Bill Cosby. And later on in my young adult life, that list grew to include Eddie Murphy, Sam Kinison, and Robin Harris. And that's my short list.

I loved to watch the classic Dean Martin and Jerry Lewis week of movies when they came on, just to watch the *physical comedic genius* of Jerry Lewis, who was the true king of that kind of physical comedy genre decades before the emergence of other brilliant comedians with similar styles like Chevy Chase and later Jim Carrey. I didn't own any rap albums like many of my friends while growing up. Instead, I had Richard Pryor, *Live on the Sunset Strip*; Eddie Murphy, *Delirious*; and other albums like *The Best of Saturday Night Live*, and bootleg cassette tapes of Redd Foxx and others from night clubs. I would even stay up late on school nights and cut off my lights in my room and act like I was asleep while I would hide my clock radio under my pillow and press my ear down on the pillow to listen to a late night radio comedy show that came on at 11:00 p.m.

Comedy was my life, and to this day there's still a lot of comedy on my internal hard drive, much of which is R-rated and not suitable for most Christian audiences. That's just the truth. I've got some good on my internal hard drive, but I'm terribly aware that everything in my heart is not good. I have *content* on my heart that requires continual purging. From the time that I was a pre-teen, I knew that I wanted to do comedy for a career, but something happened to me when I was nineteen years old that began to change the direction that I was headed in professionally.

I was a student at the time at a community college in Maryland, and although I still had my comedy career plan, I began to really sense that God was calling me to serve Him as His messenger. Now this created a huge internal civil war inside of me; because on the one hand, I wanted to make people laugh for a living, while on the other hand, I felt like God was "drafting" me into His work to be a preacher. I started negotiating with God because I knew that doing what He wanted me to do would mean I couldn't do comedy, so I said, "Well God, I'll do *clean* comedy. I won't curse, or tell crude jokes, I'll just tell 'Bill Cosby Jell-O Pudding' kinds of jokes."

However, as you can see from my bio, my negotiation didn't really work out and I did submit to the ministry call, which is why, by the grace of God, I've been preaching now for three decades. I can't say that I have any regrets about what I do, but to be quite honest with you, my interest in comedy hasn't really subsided a whole lot over the years. In fact, to this very day, every now and then, I'll get the urge to just do a stand-up comedy routine, and I'm not even joking when I say that. In fact, there are times when I'm alone out shoveling snow in the winter, that I'll literally find myself cracking up laughing at my own jokes. Although no one's around but me at those times, I find myself conflicted, feeling like the jokes shouldn't be funny to me because they are often laced with profanity.

That's what brings me back to that night in Atlanta—as I was saying, right while I was sharing how much of a blessing the trip was to me, I was also feeling one of those snow-shoveling shows coming on me that I had never done in front of a crowd. Maybe because I felt so comfortable with my staff, I just polled the group. And to make matters more dichotomous, I literally asked everyone in the room to bow their heads and close their eyes like any preacher would, and said something to the effect, "Hey y'all, if I do some comedy right now, I promise you it'll be funny, but I also need you to know that it will have some profanity in it. So if that would *offend* any of you, please just look up at me." And the funny part about that moment was the fact that a lot of the staff never looked up! Nevertheless, out of respect for those who did look up, I didn't do the routine, but in retrospect, the fact that my temperance was so weak that I would even *ask* my Church Staff for permission to be verbally profane like that was a sign that I didn't see revealing how bad a place I was in character wise at the time.

As we concluded our trip with our final night together, we all decided to have a good time talking and laughing and fellowshipping together and true to form with our staff, when we get together and we're having fun, someone will inevitably pull out board games and cards and start having a great time as we just connected together as family in a meeting room in the hotel that we had reserved. However, as the night wore on, and it went into the wee hours of the morning, and several of our team had retired to their rooms for the night, that "Snow-Shoveling Comedy Spirit" came back on me, and without warning or notice, I let loose. For a good thirty minutes or more, I just went to town, making fun of even members of my staff with profanity-laced remarks that I'm sure literally shocked some who heard it. I remember feeling like a human runaway train that couldn't be stopped because I was "on a roll," in spite of all of the damage in my wake.

I kept going because I and several others it seemed were having a great time laughing at my tirade of inappropriate humor. By the way, that's how sin works. As someone once said, "Sin will take you farther than you wanna go, keep you longer than you wanna stay, and cost you more than you wanna pay." And although many people are hurt by our sin, enough of us are having a good time that we don't often realize how much damage we're causing in the moment. So, when we returned home to Maryland, I made sure I apologized to each and every person that was in that room, just as I had apologized on other occasions when I went too far with my words in the name of being funny. As a matter of fact, on a previous trip that our staff took together, I had a similar outburst of inappropriate humor, although it wasn't profane. Yet because I felt convicted about it the next day in front of all who were there, I apologized to everyone for my behavior, in fact I even said that I was retired from making fun of people. I promised that I was done with it for good. And yet here I was again, apologizing for something that I said I wouldn't do again.

I have failed so much as a leader, and I've received so much grace from God as well. Thankfully, I'm better than I was in the areas that I've failed in. Now I didn't share that story of my failure in Atlanta because I am even the least bit proud of what I did. To the contrary, it's actually kind of hard to revisit that story because I'm so humiliated by it. But I shared the story first of all because I am absolutely clear that though I am the senior pastor of a church, I am a terribly flawed human being who is desperately in need of God's amazing grace. And I also shared my failure because it may be that you're reading this book because you probably are also aware of how fallen and depraved you are as well, and how much you, too, are in need of God's amazing grace.

I also shared it because it is an area of struggle that I have to wrestle with like we all have areas that we have to wrestle with. And in many ways, I'm making myself publicly accountable to thousands of people to make sure that I give attention to this area in my life. The final reason that I shared that story is because it's what this whole chapter is about; the importance of *controlling our mouths*. I'm convinced that there are certain parts of our human anatomy that play a role in the development and or depletion of our characters and reputations. Body parts like our *ears* and what we listen to, our *hearts* and what we have stored content-wise on our hearts, our *eyes* and what we look at, and our *feet* or the paths that we take and the places we go, and, of course, our *mouth,* is one of those body parts that have a huge impact on our characters and reputations. What I've discovered in my own life is that *what we say and avoid saying is controlled by our character.*

How This Works

Now the way this all works is fairly simple: before *words* are expressed by us verbally, they are *thoughts* in our hearts and minds. There's a period of time between a thought and the expression of that thought, and that time between those moments is when our character is at work. It may help if you imagine that character is like an internal governor that we all have inside of us. When it's strong, it will *stop* bad or unhealthy thoughts from coming out of our mouths and being expressed, and at the same time, that strong internal governor and internal control releases good thoughts that should be expressed. So whether it's saying something good, or not saying something bad, both of those "sayings" are controlled by our characters. I'm sure we'd agree that we've all said things in our lives that we wished we didn't say. The fact is, some things are better left unsaid. It's not always appropriate to "tell it like it is" or "speak our minds" or "keep it real" because everything on our mind is not worthy of communicating. In fact, some things on our minds are negative, harmful, damaging, and destructive. Therefore, there are times when silence is golden.

But there are also times when silence is violent and inconsiderate, when we intentionally withhold common courtesies like greetings to people we come into contact with or expressions of gratitude and appreciation when it's just good manners to do so. This brings us full circle to the principle that *what we say and avoid saying is controlled by our character.*

Words can do more damage than we are often aware of. And those words don't just damage those who hear them, but they also damage the very persons who say certain words. For example, words can damage reputations, which again is such a huge part of our characters. For example, people who talk as a part of their vocation, such as politicians, commentators, radio personalities, lecturers, and so forth, live under the constant scrutiny of their words. Therefore they are, in many cases, one bad choice of words away from losing their jobs and destroying their careers. In some cases, the entire body of their life's work becomes bracketed within the frame of a few, sometimes even, "off-the-record" words. In 2014, an owner of an NBA Franchise was fined $2.5 million and stripped of the ownership of his team because of some negative racial remarks that he made in a private conversation with a woman he didn't know was recording their dialogue. Ask him how important words are.

I could give one example after another of similar situations where unbridled words proved terribly costly in someone's life, and we don't have to look to radio or television to find examples of this tough lesson. Indeed, how many times have we ourselves, maybe in the midst of rage and anger or hurt, said things that we later regretted saying and were even embarrassed and sorry for saying? The problem is, even if we apologize when we say those things, the damage that it does to people as well as to our reputations is difficult to recover from, particularly, if it's something like in my case, we've said or done before. You see when people have heard it all before, even our apologies lose their value and authenticity.

I believe this principle of "what we say and avoid saying is controlled by our character" is something that had to be of importance to the father in Proverbs 4 that we've been observing because he made it part of his character-shaping speech that he gave to his son. As this father talked to his son about carrying himself in an honorable way, he told him to pay attention to the things that he hears with his ears and stores in his heart. We now pick up the conversation as the father instructs his son regarding his *mouth*. "*Put away from you a deceitful mouth, and put perverse lips far from you*" (Proverbs 4:24) NKJV We're not supposed to apply this verse *literally* and try to take our mouths off of our faces and remove our lips from above our chins. The idea is *figurative* in nature, and it's really talking about the way in which we talk and the things we say. In other words, the counsel to this son here is to not communicate in an immoral way.

There are several ways that we can apply this lesson. For example, one of the ways of making sure that we don't communicate in an immoral way is to make sure that we remove ourselves from and stay away from people that may have deceitful and perverse mouths. We do ourselves a favor by avoiding being influenced by people whose mouths are impure and immoral and insensitive and dishonest. Like the old saying goes, "Garbage in, garbage out." If we're around profanity and unhealthy dialogue a lot, then our potential for communicating in a similar fashion over time is significantly increased. So the idea here is avoid others who have foul mouths. Of course, there are certain situations where we have no control over our environments and the things that we hear, so this application has to be centered on the things that we can control and listen to.

Another way of interpreting the father's advice here to his son is to interpret it within the context of what he has just told his son to do in verse 23; making verse 24 a continuation of the thought of verse 23 where we are told to guard our hearts. The idea is that *we guard our hearts by not saying everything that is in it*. This reminds me of the Psalm that says, "May the words of my mouth, and the meditations of my heart be pleasing to You, O Lord, my Rock and my Redeemer" (Psalm 19:14 NLT). Friend, because of the fact that there is some wickedness and evil thoughts housed within all of our hearts, one of the ways that we guard our hearts is by not *expressing* those things that are *in* our hearts that are dishonorable. That means just because it's in there doesn't mean we have to say it.

Some of us say terribly offensive things and excuse it by saying, "Well, I'm just being honest. If you don't want to know the truth, don't ask me. Don't get mad at me because you can't handle the truth." On and on we go, making excuses for being reckless with our words when the reality is we can't place blame on others for our mouths being out of control because, remember, *what we say and avoid saying is controlled by our character.* And it's really our responsibility to keep harmful, thoughtless, and destructive thoughts to ourselves.

One passage in the Bible describes the human tongue as a "fire" (James 3:6). It's literally like harnessing and containing a potentially wild fire when we restrain ourselves from saying damaging things. It's not much different than when firefighters are at the scene of a house fire when not only are they there to save lives and put out the fire, but they are also there to make sure that they *contain* the fire. Containing the fire keeps it from spreading and damaging other homes and family's lives, even if the house that's on fire cannot be salvaged. Containing the fire keeps something bad from spreading. Sometimes we have *thoughts* that are as destructive as fires, and when we think those thoughts over and over again in our mind or say them to ourselves, that "fire" is doing damage to us internally on a character level. And if we are at least responsible enough to keep those destructive thoughts to ourselves, then only *our* souls will be charred by those destructive thoughts. But when we *express* those fiery and negative thoughts verbally, that fire now spreads to others, causing both the messenger and the hearers to be harmed by the *words* that are an expression of our thoughts. The mistake that we make is that we don't have enough respect for and appreciation for the huge impact that our words have on both us and those around us.

Proverbs 18:21 says that *"Death and life are in the power of the tongue."* Now that's some power right there. Our tongues can kill and heal. Our mouths have extraordinary power. Contrary to the classic but inaccurate phrase that says, "Sticks and stones may break my bones, but words will never hurt me," Proverbs 25:15b says, *". . . soft speech can break bones."* Wow! Now that's obviously figurative, but the idea is that we must not underestimate the power of our words, because words *can* hurt us, and they often do. But the same way that our words have power for destruction and injury they also have power to heal and add value, life, and joy when we use them correctly.

So again, *not* saying everything that's in our hearts, guards our hearts and ultimately our characters and reputations because although it can take years to *build* a solid character and reputation, it only takes a few seconds of reckless words to tear it down. So the idea in Proverbs 4:24 is that a deceitful mouth is a mouth that's really just out of control. It's a mouth that speaks instinctively instead of thoughtfully. It's a mouth gone wild, under the influence of ignorance and immaturity and carelessness. And it's also kind of interesting to note that the things we say and don't say have a revolving effect on our characters because, on the one hand, when our characters are strong, it helps us to govern our speech. On the other hand, when our speech is unchecked and uncontrolled and ungoverned, then that depletes, dwindles, and reduces our characters and reputation.

The truth is that both our silence and our statements are a reflection of what's going on inside of us character-wise. In other words, it's not just when I say the right thing that shows character, but it's when I hold my peace and refrain from saying the wrong thing that reveals my character as well.

What Now?

In order to apply this lesson from Proverbs 24:4 about our mouths to our lives in a character-building way, let's start by doing what my friend Johnny Parker says, "Put your mind in gear before you put your tongue on the gas." Indeed, let's think before we speak. Proverbs 29:20 says, "There is more hope for a fool than someone who speaks without thinking" (NLT). That's pretty serious. Proverbs 15:28a says, "The heart of the godly thinks carefully before speaking." So let's slow down our conversations to a thoughtful pace.

One of the classic principles from the late Stephen Covey's *Seven Habits of Highly Effective People* is to *begin with the end in mind*. The goal in that habit is to think about what the ultimate outcome is that we're seeking to attain and allow that to govern our choices and behavior in the moment. I like that, and I'd like to apply it to this chapter's lesson on controlling our mouths. The concept is, let's slow down our conversations and *speak* with the end in mind. In other words, ask yourself the question, "Is what I'm *thinking* about saying going to help me build the kind of character and reputation that my Father in Heaven would want me to have?" That's speaking with the end in mind. Here are some questions to ask yourself:

- Where will this comment or this thought ultimately take me character and reputation wise, if it is expressed?
- What will this comment do to my relationship with my child if I actually say what I'm thinking right now?
- Will what I'm about to say lead me to the kind of marriage that I want to have?
- What kind of person will people believe me to be if I state this thought on my mind right now
- Is this the way I want people to view me?

Here's the deal, you don't get to say just anything you want to say and then also control people's opinion of you after it's said. To say something immature and reckless and then get upset when people form an opinion about us based on what we said is crazy. I can't go on an angry, profanity-laced tirade and then have people with common sense think that I'm the kind of person who's always safe to be around when it comes to my response to things. I cannot go on a gossiping spree, sharing very personal information about someone else that I shouldn't share, and then after I do it, expect reasonable people to believe that they can trust me. Nope, it's not going to happen. Our words reflect our character.

The goal is to slow down our conversations and responses and to speak with the end in mind. Let's think and pray before we speak. I believe that this will not only help to build our character, which is terribly important because our character determines our future and success more than anything else, but it will also have a profoundly beneficial impact on our relationships over time. It will also immediately stop a lot of the "bleeding" that occurs in relationships where the conversations are thoughtless and reckless.

Chapter 11

Be Careful Little Eyes What You See

*"Look straight ahead, and fix your eyes on what lies before you." **Proverbs 4:25 NLT***

Why is that so many of us ride through and visit neighborhoods with homes that are way outside of our affordable price range? And then we even take it a step further, and we see a beautiful home within one of those expensive neighborhoods that's for sale, and knowing we can't afford it, we write down the phone number of the real estate agent whose name is on the "For Sale" sign so that we can inquire about the house. Why is it that we'll even make an appointment with the sales agent to see the house and walk around it imagining what it would be like to live there, saying to ourselves, *"I'll put a flat screen here, and this will be where we'll have a pool table . . ."* And on and on the fantasy goes. And even though we can't afford the house, we even take other people by the house to show them the house as well! And here's an important question: why is it that as we keep looking at the house, there are times that we eventually figure out a way, even against our better judgment, to somehow find a way to get the financing and paperwork necessary to acquire that home, even though it may very well leave us in a financial quagmire that may take decades to work our way out of if ever?

Why do some of us put a picture of our dream car in our cell phones or on the homepage of our computer screens so that we can see it every time we get on our computers or look at our cell phones? Why is it that when we do that, sooner or later we'll make a visit to a website where we can learn more about the vehicle? And why is it that eventually we'll find ourselves taking a trip to a car dealership where that vehicle is sold so that we can get inside of the vehicle and test drive it? And why is it that after a while, once our desire to own the vehicle has grown exponentially, we somehow just figure out a way to get it, even if it puts us in a compromised position financially? Why is that the case?

Why is it, especially during the winter holiday season, that some of us just innocently go to a shopping mall and see something in the window of a store that captures our attention that literally stops us in our tracks? We stand there, frozen like a deer in headlights, staring at the item that has us spellbound. And even though we told ourselves that we wouldn't buy anything extra that day because we are here to only purchase socks, we walk up to the window to get a closer look at this *amazing* thing. Why is it that once we see it up close in the window, we can't just walk away, but instead we tell whoever we're shopping with, "give me a minute and I'll meet you in the food court"? Meanwhile we go *inside* the store (for just a moment of course) to *investigate* a little bit. "How much does it cost?" we ask. "Are there any in stock in my size? Do you have it in navy blue?"

Why is it that we can go from, "I'm not here for that," to figuring out a way to purchase it, thinking, "Maybe if I can get the sales rep to hold the item for me for a few days until I get my next paycheck, then I'll have enough financial wiggle room to make it work." Whether we end up using cash, or using "cap space" on an already abusively used credit card, why do we make purchases like that even though we don't really need the item and we really can't afford it? Why is that?

If I can take my line of questioning a little deeper, why is it that some of us have been "scoping out" *someone*? We've been looking intently at someone that we find attractive, whether we're seeing them for the first time and we can't stop staring at them, or we've been checking them out for a while now. Maybe we've been sneaking peeks at them from time to time—an occasional glance and a smile here or there. In fact, maybe we're wondering if they feel the same way about us, as we do about them. And why is it that even though actually hooking up with this person could compromise our integrity, our reputation, our family, our ministry, our testimony, and even some close friendships, just the sight of this person and our constant attention paid to them has us moving closer and closer to reasoning our way into making the connection and initiating the hookup? Why does stuff like that happen?

Well, there's an old wise king in antiquity who I believe helps to answer all of these questions in a simple yet powerful way. His name is King Solomon and here are his words: "... The eye never has enough of seeing." (Ecclesiastes 1:8 NIV). This same king also once said that, "Death and Destruction are never satisfied, and neither are human eyes." (Proverbs 27:20 NIV). Wow.

One of the problems that you and I face anatomically is the fact that our eyes are vitally connected to our moral compass and character. Therefore, if we are dissatisfied internally, our eyes won't be capable of looking at something enticing and remaining content with *only seeing* it. They will lead us to want to *experience* and to *have* what we're seeing. The truth is we've *all* had our eyes focused on something or even someone that may have taken us somewhere that we shouldn't have gone or led us to make a decision we shouldn't have made. The problem with staring at the wrong thing in particular, is the fact that the eye is not satisfied with seeing, no matter what it is that we are seeing. Our eyes are never satisfied. Therefore, what we continue to see, we may eventually want to seize. So as the classic childhood song aptly says, "Be careful little eyes what you see."

How This Works

The Indiana University Medical School did a study on the effects of how what we look at for an extended period of time can have an impact on us mentally. They used forty-four teenagers for the study, and let them do something they all loved doing—playing video games. They all got to play a video game for thirty minutes. Twenty-two of the teens played a car-racing game called "Need for Speed," and the other twenty-two teens played a moderately violent war video game called "Medal of Honor." (They chose not to use some of the more graphically violent video games on the market at the time, and instead went with "Medal of Honor" because it was rated moderate, and it was also rated for teenagers.)

They let these forty-four kids have at it and play their respective game for thirty minutes and immediately tested their brain activity with an MRI following the game. Interestingly enough, the kids who played the teenage-rated, moderately violent war game had more brain activity in the part of the brain that controls emotional arousal than the kids who played the car racing game. Furthermore, their study showed that the kids who played the teenage-rated, moderately violent war game had less brain activity in the part of the brain that manages their inhibition, concentration, and self-control than the kids who played the racing game.[3] Now, even though the study didn't go so far as to claim that violence in our communities can be directly linked to the amount of violence that an individual consumes *visually,* what the evidence did bear out is the fact that observing even moderate violence for thirty minutes does something to the human brain that's not good. It made these teenagers psychologically less self-controlled, more impulsive, and more emotionally aroused.

The reality is, when we *look* at something or someone for a long enough time, it can have an effect on us psychologically even if we're not conscious of it. Therefore, what we look at for extended periods of time can ultimately affect our character because of its impact on our mood, our brains, and potentially our behavior.

What the study above also proves is that in order for something that we see to impact us on a level that's deeper than just our vision, it requires us to look at it for a sustained period of time. So I'd like to make a distinction between *glancing* at something and *gazing* at something. A glance can be innocent or accidental, but a gaze is a sustained staring at or studying of something. It is looking with intention and even enjoyment or pleasure. It didn't just pass by, it lingered, and although a glance might not impact us on a character level, a gaze can, and in my personal experience it doesn't take an entire thirty minutes for that to happen. Consequently, since what we look at for extended periods of time can ultimately affect our character, we must avoid gazing at anything that soils our character.

Again, there's a difference between gazing at something and glancing at it. Things come into our vision and view all the time, and that's normal and natural. To pause and *intentionally* observe something for a period of time is to gaze on it, and that's when our characters become exposed to what we're seeing. So we need to keep our eyes away from things that would *soil* our character.

Another reason why it is so important that we take personal responsibility for avoiding the temptation to gaze at anything that soils our character is because in addition to all of the examples that I gave above about how gazing at things can eventually impact our decisions, such as purchasing an expensive home, car, fashion item, and so forth, another reality that we are dealing with is the fact that by and large the entertainment industry and world of media is really not concerned about our character. They're concerned about our attraction, our enticement, and whatever appeals to us. The fashion industry, for example, in general is not concerned about designing clothing that is character-friendly. Instead, clothes are designed to be trendy, fashionable, and often sexy. The majority of films that are made in the film industry are not made to protect and preserve our character. Films are made to entertain. Therefore, the more skin, the more sex, the more opportunities to make heroes out of a man who can kill many men in a flurry of violence, the greater the wow factor, and subsequently, the bigger the box office results.

The challenging work of avoiding putting our focus and attention and gaze on things that soil our character is really an upstream swim, especially in the time period in which we live. There was a time when the governing bodies that sensor television shows, especially, were a lot more character-sensitive. For example, there was a time when I was a kid that you wouldn't see a man and a woman in bed together on television, even if they were married. I remember as a kid watching *The Dick Van Dyke Show* and the *I Love Lucy* show, and even married couples on those shows slept in separate beds; and every bedroom scene had them dressed in full length, long-sleeved pajamas. Nowadays on television, whether you're married or not, or even an adult or not, bedroom scenes are far more sexual than what was once legally allowed on television. And the envelope continues to be pushed.

I'm not saying that we shouldn't watch television or ever go to the movies, but I am saying that what we consistently take in with our eyes *will* have an impact on the purity of our character, for better or worse. I think it's a mistake to be laissez-faire with our television and movie watching as well as with our Internet surfing if we're going to pay attention to our character. If indeed character matters and it is what determines our future and success more than anything else, then we have to avoid gazing at things that will soil our characters. Again, the danger of gazing at what's coming out of Hollywood in particular is the fact that as I heard author Josh McDowell say, "Hollywood only shows one side of things too often," which makes much of what we see so misleading and deceptive. For example, Hollywood shows violence and killing in a way that kind of makes it seem heroic at times. Without our being really cognizant of it, there are times that, if we have an affinity towards the movie character that's doing the killing in the movie, we'll even applaud or feel a sense of mission accomplished when our "hero" blows somebody up.

The problem is, what Hollywood doesn't show us enough is the ravaging effects that violence has on surviving family members in the real lives of both the offenders and the victims. Hollywood doesn't spend a lot of time showing scenes of family members receiving a phone call from the police department, saying that their loved one has been involved in a shooting and they need to get to the hospital immediately. Hollywood doesn't spend a lot of time during its *glorification* of violence, showing grief-stricken family members identifying the remains of a loved one, whose life was ended tragically and much too soon. Hollywood doesn't usually elaborate on the generational effects of violence when one person is murdered and their life is cut off, and the one who committed the crime is cut off from society for the rest of their lives in prison. They do not show the affects that has on what both people could have become and were supposed to do with their lives.

Moreover, when Hollywood shows its plethora of sex, you don't see a lot of people going through the pain and embarrassment of an unplanned pregnancy and how two people, who don't even have a covenanted, marital commitment to each other, are now responsible for raising a child. Hollywood doesn't show how grandparents often become primary caregivers of many innocent children and thus have their lives adjusted to this new normal. You don't see a lot of scenes of people in waiting rooms of health clinics in pain and ashamed because they've contracted a sexually transmitted disease, some of which are incurable and even life-threatening. Hollywood *will show* the *pleasure* that an unfaithful spouse is having while committing adultery, but rarely will it show the devastation and depression of the other spouse once it's discovered or the loneliness and dysfunction of children who are often left behind because somebody said, "I'm going to do what makes *me* happy." Friends, Hollywood doesn't come *close* to measuring how much that kind of happiness costs.

As we continue reading what this wise father was teaching his son in Proverbs 4 about the anatomy of character, I wasn't surprised when he made sure he talked about the impact that his son's eyes and what he gazed at would have on his character. Indeed, it's not just important that we pay attention to the things we hear with our ears, and what we house in our hearts, and what we herald from our mouths, it is also critical to be careful regarding what we hone in on with our eyes. Here's the father's advice in Proverbs 4:25: *"Let your eyes look straight ahead, fix your gaze directly before you ." NIV* Now by way of application, this verse could be used as a pep talk or motivational speech on staying focused in life. Look straight ahead. Keep your eyes on the prize. Keep your eyes on the goal ahead. Don't look to the left or to the right; don't even look back. Just stay focused. And that's certainly not a *bad* application of this verse of scripture. But when you view this verse from a *character* perspective, the verse takes on a whole different meaning.

I believe that this verse on a character level is warning us about the use of our eyes just like the previous verses in this section of Proverbs 4 have warned us about the influence of other body parts on our character. This verse is warning us of the danger of setting our gaze and attention on the wrong things. And therefore we must avoid gazing at anything or anyone, for that matter, that soils our character. By the way, getting in trouble for staring and gazing at the wrong things is not new at all. In fact, it's gotten a lot of people in the Bible in trouble, like Eve for example, in Genesis 3. Eve was looking at fruit on a tree that she was not supposed to eat because God said that if anyone ate the fruit on *that* tree they would die. In Genesis 3:4–6 the serpent came to Eden and basically said to Eve, "Don't take that warning from God about this tree serious. C'mon Eve; let's be realistic. If you eat this fruit, *you're not going to die.* God just doesn't want you to eat it because if you eat it you'll be like Him knowing good and evil."

So with that demonic perspective in mind, instead of staring at *forbidden fruit,* Eve is now staring at "power," which is one of the ways that temptation deceives us. When we first look at something that is forbidden, we are sometimes aware that it's forbidden initially. But as we continue to stare, our opinion about it or them changes, which makes what we're looking at more desirable. Remember, "The eye is never satisfied with just seeing." So when the serpent said these words to Eve, it stirred up something in Eve as she continued looking at this forbidden fruit and her hunger for the *power* that this food would give her. Eventually Eve ate the fruit, and it all started with her *eyes* (Be careful little eyes what you see). The effects of Eve's decision are still being experienced today.

There was also a man in the Bible named Achan in Joshua 7, whom God told, along with the Israelites, to go into a particular city and conquer it. God also told them to make sure they didn't touch the sacred things that they might find there. However, Achan chose to disobey that command from God, and as a result of Achan's decision, Israel suffered loss of life and resources in a subsequent battle, and Achan and his family were eventually stoned to death and set on fire as a judgment against him for his sin. Listen to how Achan himself said it all happened, in Joshua 7:20–21:

> Achan replied, "It is true! I have sinned against the Lord, the God of Israel. Among the plunder I *saw* a beautiful robe from Babylon, 200 silver coins, and a bar of gold weighing more than a pound. *I wanted them so much that I took them.* They are hidden in the ground beneath my tent, with the silver buried deeper than the rest. (NLT)

Achan's problems all started with his eyes (Be careful little eyes what you see). He said, "I *saw* a beautiful robe." And after listing what he saw, notice the next thing he says, "*I wanted them so much that I took them.*" His gaze led him to grab something forbidden. What if, when he saw those things, he swiftly appreciated their beauty and value and turned away from them because he knew they were off limits? It would've saved his life and the life of his family and so many others from the trouble that his decision caused them. Be careful little eyes what you see.

There was a popular king in the Bible named David who also got in trouble when his eyes gazed at someone forbidden in 2 Samuel 11. He saw from his palace rooftop a married woman named Bathsheba taking a bath, and after staring at her, he inquired about her. Even after finding out that she was someone else's wife, his lust, fueled by what he saw, had taken over his ability to reason properly and make good decisions because, remember, the eye is never satisfied with just seeing. His eyes gazed on someone and something that eventually soiled his character. David subsequently used his power to have Bathsheba brought to him, he had sexual intercourse with her, impregnated her, and later had her husband killed as a part of his efforts to cover up his sin. David set in motion a myriad of traumas in his own family and another family as a result of his decision, including incest, rape, murder, and a domestic revolt against his throne led by his son. All of these tragic consequences were the result of a sin that started with his *eyes*. (Be careful little eyes what you see.)

Now I may be saying what I'm about to say because I'm a man, but I believe that sexual temptation of the eyes is especially something that we as men are vulnerable to. It's been well documented that men are visually stimulated and visually oriented. There are things that we have to avoid gazing at because if it's something that God doesn't want us to have, but we continue to gaze at it, the temptation to have it will continue to grow. Once again, the eye is never satisfied with just seeing. The serpent (Satan) is still working to get our eyes locked on something or someone inappropriate; his plot and plan is for our ultimate humiliation and destruction. That is why watching pornography, for example, is so dangerous; it's a trap. I've often said that pornography is a sliding board to Hell. It's a deceptive vice. How? Seeing the wrong thing often enough will lead to further deviant behavior. And after a while, seeing is not enough.

Any person, who has committed adultery or hired a prostitute or committed a sexual crime, at some point was looking or gazing at something or someone inappropriate. Because the eye is never satisfied with just seeing, our eyes led the way into some destructive behavior. This is why we *must* avoid gazing at anything or anybody that soils our character; gazing at certain things will feed our appetites for it. It drives us towards it. That is why the father in Proverbs 4 had to have this part of the character talk with his son because of the fact that the eye is never satisfied. So this father tells his son, "Son, let your eyes look straight ahead, and fix your gaze directly before you." Why? Because our character is affected by the things we look at.

Our gaze and our godliness are synced together. If we continue to study and look at that which is forbidden, then we are on our way to a sad, destructive, costly end. Jesus Christ is so adamant about this whole matter of guarding what we gaze at with our eyes that He said in Matthew 5:27–29:

> "You have heard that it was said to those of old, 'You shall not commit adultery.' But I say to you that whoever looks

at a woman to lust for her has already committed adultery with her in his heart. If your right eye causes you to sin, pluck it out and cast it from you; for it is more profitable for you that one of your members perish, than for your whole body to be cast in hell." NKJV

Jesus says if you've got a gazing with your eye at the wrong-thing problem, then pluck your eye out and throw it away. Now obviously, if we take a literal application to that passage (which we shouldn't), we'd all more than likely just have left eyes because He said pluck out the right one. I think the point that Jesus is making is we must pay attention to what we are paying unhealthy attention to and deal *aggressively* with it. Too often our problem is we do nothing aggressive about the sins of our eyes. We don't "pluck it out" by going the other way, walking in another direction, or staying away from that environment. We don't change the channel or "turn the other cheek" and look the other way. Instead, too often, we just take it all *in*. And we have to understand that our eyes are the doorways through which we download things onto our character hard drives. And if it's the wrong stuff, it will soil our character. Therefore, Jesus says to deal with that stuff *aggressively*.

What Now?

How can we *apply* this lesson in a character-building way? Well for starters, we can make sure that we keep something good and positive in front of our eyes each day. Reading good, godly, character-building material on a regular basis is a good way of cleansing and building our character. Another thing we can do is to make a covenant with our eyes as a man in the Bible named Job did. "I have made a covenant with my eyes not to look at a woman with lust" (Job 31:1 NIV). Now even though Job was specifically making a covenant with *his* eyes not to look at a *woman* with lust, we all have something or someone that we can look at that would soil our characters. So *our* commitment may be making a covenant with our eyes to not look at some material thing that we will eventually covet and go after even though it's not something we can afford. It may be covenanting with our eyes not to look at someone and what they have and feeding our desire to have what they have instead of appreciating and being grateful for what we have, which can also affect our characters. So make the covenant with your eyes that you need to specifically make around the things or people that tempt you to look at.

Psalm 101:3a says, "I will set nothing wicked before my eyes." (NKJV) That means I will look at nothing on television, on the Internet, on my cell phone, my iPad, my laptop, my desktop, magazines, or on social media that tempts me. Nothing. Again, gazing is different than glancing. Gazing is a sustained look. It's *viewing* something for an extended period of time to take it all in. It's intentional, not accidental or coincidental. It's thinking about it in an inappropriate way. If something crosses your path or sight line, you can't always prevent that from happening but you can turn away if it's something that will soil your character. As the old saying goes, "You can't stop a bird from flying over your head, but you can stop it from building a nest there."

We have to covenant with our eyes that we will not gaze upon anything or anyone that will soil our characters. Turn it off. Walk the other way. Look the other way. Change the channel. Now some of us, who may have been feeding our flesh and our souls improperly through visually staring at the wrong things, will find this change to be very difficult. Therefore it will definitely take support and accountability to overcome this challenge. In fact, it will feel like going through a drug or alcohol detoxification process. Fight through it anyway, because your purity of character is worth the fight.

For some people, it will be an awakening to things that maybe you weren't conscious of because they seemed so innocent, but were actually soiling your character. Heed these fresh new warnings and reverse the course that you're on. For others, getting good content and good things in front of us will also have an enormous and positive impact on our characters as well. Here are a few extra things we can do to help solidify this very important character-building process.

For one, don't try to climb this mountain alone. Reach out for accountability and support. If you don't live alone, start making sure that you go to bed at a reasonable hour, particularly when everyone else goes to bed because typically most people find themselves looking at forbidden things when they're up late at night and everyone is asleep. Therefore, they don't have any accountability, which is probably one reason why most X-rated programming comes on late at night.

Turn off all electronic devices after a certain hour, particularly during the times of the evening when you know you'll be most tempted to look at something inappropriate. Also, if you live with other people, keep your laptop out in an open area at all times where anyone can see what sites you're visiting, and give your spouse your pass codes so that he/she can always check your history on your phone and your laptops. Make yourself accountable and make sinning with your eyes harder for you. Whether you live alone or with other people, get an accountability app on all of your electronic devices with filters that will not only prevent you from looking at inappropriate material, but will also notify people who hold you accountable if and when you do. If you're in a small group or you've got some trusted friends and confidantes, let them know your struggle and ask for their prayers and support and encouragement and accountability.

Finally, here's a tool that I learned from psychologist and author Dr. Douglas Weiss. He suggests in his writings that to break addictive behaviors that we wear a *rubber band* on our wrist that will serve as a powerful aid in adjusting our behavior. Dr. Weiss says that we can recondition or retrain our brains through this simple but effective behavior modification exercise. Here's how it works. Whenever we *see* something or someone that is off limits or forbidden (something or someone that, if we continue to stare, could eventually soil our character). When that happens, in addition to turning away from what we're looking at, at that moment, we also pop our wrists with the rubber band, introducing pain to our brains in association with what we just saw, and also making a positive statement like, "I'm a one-woman man." Or, "I'm grateful for what God has given to me, and I don't want what belongs to someone else." "My body is God's temple and I will not defile it." This is a form of classical conditioning that will serve us well in developing visual discipline and stronger characters in our lives. For example, Dr. Weiss says,

> "If you have a dog that continually has "accidents" on the floor of your house, and every time it happens you give that dog a doggie treat, eventually that dog will associate going to the bathroom on the floor as a prelude to a reward. And you'll end up having a very fat dog, and a very messy house. But if instead you responsibly swat the dog with a newspaper when it messes on the floor,

eventually that dog will associate messing the floor with pain and punishment and therefore will be trained not to do it."

That's how the rubber band technique works. Instead of "rewarding" ourselves when we see a seductive picture or video or image of a woman by masturbating and therefore associate gazing at something or someone inappropriate as pleasurable, we must instead introduce a painful consequence into the equation, turn away, pop our wrists with the rubber band, and that will eventually retrain our brains to view the wrong thing the right way. And if consistent, the rubber band snapping technique will take anywhere from thirty to ninety days before you won't even need it anymore because your brain has been retrained (although some people continue to wear it, just in case they find themselves slipping again).

Listen, it takes a lot of work to fight and resist visual temptation, but it's a battle worth fighting because our character is at stake. Having a healthy and clean character is critical because it is our character that determines our future and our success more than anything else. So here's to visual victories in our lives.

CHAPTER 12

FAILING TO PLAN IS PLANNING TO FAIL

*"²⁶Mark out a straight path for your feet; stay on the safe path.²⁷Don't get sidetracked; keep your feet from following evil." **Proverbs 4:26-27 NLT***

On February 11, 1990, in Tokyo, Japan, one of the most shocking moments in professional sports history took place. On that day, a relatively unknown boxer from Columbus, Ohio not only defeated the heavyweight champion of the world at the time, but he convincingly knocked the champion out. James "Buster" Douglas was the unsung fighter from Ohio, and the infamous "Iron" Mike Tyson was the larger-than-life champion that he knocked out in the tenth round of their title bout to become the undisputed heavyweight boxing champion of the world. Amazing. Now just in case you don't follow the sport of boxing, let me explain to you why what happened that night was so surprising.

Mike Tyson had never been beaten before as a professional boxer. He was undefeated. In fact, no one had really ever come close to beating him. His record leading up to his fight with Buster Douglas was 37–0 and 33 of those 37 wins came as a result of Tyson knocking out his opponent. He was without question the most dominant and feared athlete in his sport.

Douglas on the other hand was a much less heralded fighter. He was a relative journeyman boxer, and he'd never even faced an opponent of

Mike Tyson's caliber in his entire boxing career. In fact, the consensus of opinion regarding who would win the fight between these two was so lopsided that no one really gave Douglas a fighting chance (no pun intended). In fact, the expected outcome of the Douglas-Tyson fight was such a no-brainer that only one betting entity, the Mirage Casino in Las Vegas, even made betting possible on the fight, and they had Tyson favored to win the fight at the staggering odds of 42–1. You have to understand that Mike Tyson had developed such a reputation of destroying his opponents that the question was never about him losing; the question was always how long could his opponent hold him and run from him before he finally knocked them out?

Yet, against all odds, on February 11, 1990, Buster Douglas did the unthinkable. He didn't just beat Mike Tyson; he beat him up and knocked him out. But *how?* What happened? How in the world did David beat Goliath that day? How did James Buster Douglas shock the world? How did the mighty fall on that day? How did Mike Tyson, who had never even been knocked *down* before in his professional career get knocked *out* that day? Was it a conspiracy? Was the fight fixed? Did Tyson take a dive? Was Douglas on steroids?

Well, the answer for the most part is kind-of simple. James Douglas did something *before* the fight that Mike Tyson didn't do nearly as well. Douglas *trained* for the fight and trained hard. He prepared himself for the fight with Mike Tyson as if he were facing his greatest opponent ever, and indeed he was. He worked hard in the gym, got himself into excellent condition, and fought a fight that was perfect for counteracting the style of Mike Tyson. Douglas had an experienced trainer as well, who *studied* Mike Tyson through films of his previous fights and prepared Douglas thoroughly using a strategy and fight plan that inevitably beat him. To put it bluntly, James Buster Douglas was prepared.

On the other hand, Mike Tyson trained and prepared for the fight with Buster Douglas as if Douglas would simply be another notch in his belt. Tyson's prefight training regimen for the year leading up to the Buster Douglas fight was described by Dr. Gil Clancy as including a lot of "loose living." In fact, Mike Tyson's discipline as a professional fighter had taken a turn downhill about two years prior to the Douglas fight, when Tyson fired his long-time trainer Kevin Rooney and replaced him with an inexperienced trainer. Kevin Rooney was one of Tyson's original corner men who began working with him when he first started boxing. Rooney was also the last link that Tyson had in his inner circle of influencers that were connected to Cus D'Amato, Tyson's childhood and young adult mentor. It was D'Amato who first taught Tyson how to box, and he, along with Rooney, groomed Tyson into the ferocious fighter that he had become.

Boxing experts say that once Tyson fired Rooney, he clearly abandoned the original "peek-a-boo" style of fighting that he had, with head movement, defensive skills, and vicious body attacks that he would unleash on his opponents. Instead, Tyson began to resign himself to attempting to be a head-hunting-only, one-punch knockout artist. This proved to be detrimental to his success. Not only had Mike Tyson chosen to part ways with his long-time trainer, Kevin Rooney, before his fight with Buster Douglas, but less than one year before the Douglas fight, Tyson's rocky marriage to Actress Robin Givens was ended in a divorce that hurt him profoundly on an emotional level and cost him millions of dollars financially in the process. And if those were not enough unproductive changes, in addition to that drama in his life, during that same time period Tyson was involved in a street fight with another professional fighter named Mitch Green in which Tyson broke his hand. This was all leading up to the Buster Douglas fight. But that's not all. Mike Tyson was also dealing with a number of legal challenges and other shenanigans that accompanied the business relationship that he had with notorious boxing promoter Don King.

So with a new but certainly unimproved fighting style, a new and inexperienced trainer (about whom I'll say more momentarily), a broken heart, poor preparation (in fact, he was knocked down by one of his sparring partners during his training camp), and a life that was spiraling out of control emotionally, relationally, domestically, financially, and professionally, Mike Tyson stepped into the ring with a man who had worked his butt off to prepare himself for that moment. And when you have all of those ingredients together, you have the recipe for a disaster for Mike Tyson.

Time and space in this chapter won't permit me to take you round by round through that unforgettable fight, but let me briefly take you into a defining moment in the fight to highlight the conundrum that Mike Tyson was in. During the fight, Tyson's left eye began to swell as a result of the punishment that he had taken in the fight at the hands of Douglas. Again, because he had fired Kevin Rooney his trainer, he had an entirely new crew in his corner. There was one glaring problem with this new crew—they didn't know what they were doing! They were totally unprepared to deal with the circumstances on several fronts. For example, they didn't really know what to tell this heroic figure whom they lauded when he was surprisingly getting pummeled in the fight. At that point, he really didn't need "fans" in his corner; he needed a wise, savvy boxing coach and trainer who could help him understand what kind of adjustments he needed to make.

Furthermore, in addition to this corner's inability to challenge, coach, correct, and motivate Tyson, when his eye swelled to the point where he couldn't see out of it, his corner did something that would be hilarious if it wasn't so sad. Whenever a fighter has facial swelling, particularly vision-impairing swelling, that fighter is in danger of experiencing more punishment, partly because he cannot see the punches coming in order to block them or get out of the way of them. So what professional, trained corner-men do in those situations is they use a very cold metal device called an Endswell that is placed over the swelling with great pressure to literally end the swelling. Well of course, given the fact that Mike Tyson was a 42–1 favorite to win the fight, I guess his new corner crew didn't see the need to even have an Endswell device on hand. So not only do they not have a clue what to tell him to stop the beating, but they don't have the tools needed to help treat the beating between rounds either. So here's what they did: they sent someone to get ice for them, and they *made an ice bag* by putting ice in a latex glove that one of them had, and they put this emergency ice pack on his eye between rounds.

So suffice it to say, Mike Tyson's eye continued to swell because such a creative device wouldn't work fast enough to treat his swelling. That's not to mention the fact that as the ice was melting in the latex glove, air and water were accumulating in it, and instead of draining the glove periodically of the air and water and refilling it with fresh ice, they continued to use the same glove over and over again until it was nothing more than a mushy cold-water balloon. To watch it felt more like you were watching a sit-com, than the heavyweight championship of the world.

Now in order to reduce swelling around the eye, significant pressure must be placed on the swelling with something cold and solid, and the swelling must be literally pushed away from the eye. But none of this was happening in Tyson's corner; in fact, the latex glove, turned-ice-bag, turned cool-water-balloon, was just gently placed against the side of Mike

Tyson's face. With all the other things that Tyson was competing against, he was now also fighting with the ability to only see out of one eye. So not only was Tyson unprepared *before* the fight based on how he trained, but apparently his crew was unprepared *during* the fight based on how they responded to crises. All of this led to what is arguably one of the greatest upsets in boxing history. So how did Buster Douglas shock the world? It was by doing something every day for months that his opponent wasn't doing—preparing himself well for the fight. Neither one of those men got into shape *during* the fight. No, the fight *revealed* what kind of shape they were already in.

We all have "opponents" that we have to face in life that require preparation to face successfully. If we are unprepared, we will be defeated by those opponents, such as a temptation that challenges our greed or an opportunity to be in an improper relationship or an invitation to participate in something that's morally wrong. We all have opponents that we have to face in life, so we have to be prepared to face them. What determines whether or not we are prepared to face these opponents is the strength of our character.

How This Works

Our character is something that we have to work on every day because inevitably we will walk into the ring against an opponent that we cannot beat if we don't. Whatever that "opponent" is in your life and mine, when it shows up, the opponent doesn't *build* our character, it *reveals* what kind of character we've been developing up until that point. Many of us have taken some tough losses in our lives because we were defeated by something that our character wasn't strong enough to fight. Therefore, it is imperative that our characters be developed, trained, and built up on a daily basis. Unfortunately there's no character injection we can take or a character drink that we can chug down or pick up from the Vitamin Shoppe to fast-track our character development. Character takes a daily focus and discipline to develop.

The one character development emphasis that I'd like to focus on in this chapter is this: *we must establish a thoughtful and prayerful plan of actions and interactions every day*. To establish a thoughtful and prayerful plan of actions and interactions each day is a very character-friendly exercise. I want to emphasize "each day" because character building is a daily exercise. We can't build our character in one day, but we can build it day by day. And that's a wise thing for us to do because sadly enough, our character and reputation can be demolished in one day because of a poor decision. So every day we need to take some time to thoughtfully and prayerfully plan our actions and interactions because our character is built day by day.

Now the reason why it's so important when it comes to training and developing our character that we go through a thoughtful and prayerful process every day, regarding that day's actions and interactions, is because whenever we don't do that we become reaction-driven in our lives instead of purpose-driven. Whenever we are reaction driven, we tend to respond to things in an immature way. But if we take the time to daily prepare ourselves, then we can respond to things with the end goal in mind. Furthermore, we need to establish a thoughtful and prayerful plan of actions and interactions each day because we're not going to become the kind of character-strong person that we ultimately want to be by accident. Just like no one can become or remain the heavyweight champion of the world by accident, no one accidentally develops integrity and strength of character. No one accidentally develops honesty and self-control. No one accidentally develops wisdom and sound decision-making skills. No one accidentally develops the humility to admit their wrongs, own their mistakes, and ask for forgiveness.

Character development happens intentionally. You have to plan to live above reproach. You have to prepare ahead of time to do and say the right things. This is actually the advice that the father we've been looking at in Proverbs 4 gives to his son in verses 26–27: "Mark out a straight path for your feet; stay on the safe path. Don't get sidetracked; keep your feet from following evil" (NLT). Now on the surface, it would appear that a very basic application for this passage would be to take it as a challenge to stay out of negative environments. In other words, by keeping your feet from following evil, the application is to stay away from nightclubs, strip clubs, casinos, bars, and any other place that would smear your testimony. But the verse is not that simple.

Notice that the father's emphasis up front in verse 26 is on his son *pre-planning* or *thinking through* the path that he will walk. And make sure (son), that your journey is safe. Now whenever you see words in poetical biblical literature like "path" or "walk," those words can be used inter-changeably with the words "conduct" or "lifestyle." Our "path," as it is used in the Bible, is a reference to the way we conduct our lives. It's not just the places we go but also the decisions we make and the relationships and interactions we have, as well. So the emphasis in verse 26 is all about thoughtfully contemplating and laying out a safe life map and strategy.

In verse 27, the emphasis is on warning the son of the consequences of not doing verse 26. It will cause you to get "sidetracked." It'll cause you to drift or swerve off course and thus have yourself and your "feet" caught up in evil. Therefore, by doing verse 26 that is really to *establish a thoughtful and prayerful plan of actions and interactions each day,* we protect ourselves from veering off of that established, "marked-out," preplanned path, and we're actually keeping our feet and our lives from following evil. So this father is telling his son that you need to think about where you're going before you go in verse 26. It's not always wise to just go with the flow or just go wherever the wind blows us. Instead you must "mark out" or plan your journey because thinking about where you're going before you go increases the odds that your journey will have safety and stability. On the other hand when we're unsure about where we're headed, it makes our life's journey challenging and difficult.

It's like someone driving a car while lost. They go way below the speed limit and make erratic turns and lane changes while frustrating other drivers. In fact, drivers who are confused about where they're going are more at risk to get into and cause accidents. And when we don't have a thoughtful and prayerful plan of actions and interactions for each day, we sort of meander about aimlessly through life and the danger in doing this is it can land us in an evil, unsafe place. So just as drivers are able to drive more safely and confidently when they know where they're going, we can do the same when we have an internal navigation system that has prayer-fully and carefully thought through and planned out our daily actions and interactions.

In my opinion, the very best way of planning our daily actions and interactions is by using the Bible to be our GPS. Psalm 119:105 says, *"Your word is a lamp to my feet And a light to my path." NKJV* What a gift the Scriptures are to us because there are so many things about life that are unclear and uncertain. When our pathways are gray, fuzzy, cloudy, or even dark, we need a light that illumines our path, and the Bible is that light and that lamp that directs our steps. Psalm 119:133 says, *"Order my steps in thy word..." KJV* We need God's daily direction in our lives because He knows where all of the traps and minefields are. I think that it's not only important to have short-term and long-term plans and goals for our lives, but we also need to have daily plans as well. What I do in each day is going to determine where I ultimately end up in the future, no matter how lofty my vision and goals for my future may be. What I do day in and day out is what will determine where I go in life.

The father concludes his advice for his son in verse 27 by telling him, "Don't get sidetracked." Don't get distracted from the safe path in verse 26 and end up on the evil path in verse 27. The best way to stay tethered to the right path and away from the wrong path is by thoughtfully and prayerfully preplanning our actions and interactions each day.

What Now?

In order to thoughtfully and prayerfully plan our daily actions and interactions, we have to make sure that we wake up early enough to have time in the morning to carry out this discipline before we get into the hustle and bustle of our days. Having a regular time in the morning for prayer, reading, and writing our daily plans is critical to us not swerving into evil. We have to build that into our days. This requires waking up early enough to get this time in. Waking up early is more realistic when we go to bed early. Therefore, my suggestion is a bedtime of around 10:00 p.m. or earlier and a wake-up time of somewhere between 5:00 a.m. and 6:00 a.m., depending upon what time your workday begins. Waking up early is essential to this discipline and character-producing habit, and those who habitually sleep as long and as late as they can, only getting up in just enough time just to make it to the job or an appointment, have to change that habit.

I try to journal my prayers, read the Bible, and read from at least one other helpful book for at least one hour to begin each day. I've seen a huge difference in my life over the years when I consistently do this, as well as when I don't do it regularly. It has a huge impact on my character and my actions and interactions. The fact is, we are where we are because of the habits and disciplines that we've practiced that impact our character. If you are satisfied with where you are spiritually, professionally, physically, financially, and relationally, then don't change a thing. Just make sure you maintain your current character building practices and disciplines without stopping or you will experience character atrophy. But if you're not totally content with where you are in those areas and others, then making the investment of developing our character on a daily basis is a small change that will pay off in huge dividends down the road.

I opened this chapter telling you what happened in sports on February 11, 1990. Even if you don't follow professional boxing, you may know that Mike Tyson never regained the prominence or success in the ring that he had before he fought James Buster Douglas. It was all downhill for Mike after that. But there's something else you need to know. As good as Buster Douglas was for the months leading up to his fight with Mike Tyson and as good as he was the night that he fought Mike Tyson, it all went downhill for him after that fight as well. The hard work that Douglas was putting in every day to prepare for his fight with Mike Tyson didn't continue afterward. Less than nine months later, in October 1990, Buster Douglas was knocked out in the third round of his first and only heavyweight title defense against Evander Holyfield. In fact, not only was James Douglas not consistent in his training, but some years later his body weight ballooned up to 400 pounds, and he almost died in a diabetic coma.

How do you go from being lean enough and physically fit enough to beat Iron Mike Tyson when he was undefeated, to almost eating yourself to death? You can get there by not doing consistently what made you successful. You want to know why we need to work on our character every day for the rest of our lives? It's because character atrophies when it's not developed.

CHAPTER 13

THE REWARD

There's no doubt that this book requires a lot of work and introspection to the person who's in need of a second chance. And although leaders especially might find this book helpful it's also very challenging and sometimes the work might eclipse the rewards. Indeed with all of the work involved in a leader recovering from a moral failure, sometimes it's easy to miss all of the benefits that come as a result of it. Here are some of the benefits that leaders, who by the grace of God, the loving, consistent support of family and friends, and the forgiveness of even those they let down and led, have enjoyed.

A Better Marriage

Many leaders who stumble into reckless decision-making usually have a level of unhealthy estrangement in their marriages. One of the first things that's addressed in comprehensive counseling and therapy is this critical and fragmented relationship. Many "recovered" leaders have dynamic, fun-filled, loving, renewed, and passionate marriages. In fact, their marriages are a safe barometer moving forward to measure how safe they are to lead. Be assured if he is unable to successfully relate to one person at home, then he is certainly going to be off-kilter when it comes to managing the dozens of relationships within the organization that he leads. Therefore, many leaders who've recovered from failure and/

or indiscretion are now more fit to lead than ever, primarily because their marriages are healthier and more unified than ever.

A Sober Lifestyle

Many leaders who've "fallen," as I've shared in this book, have grappled with some form of addiction that they turned to for comfort or they felt entitled to partake in. However, once exposed, treated, and restored, those leaders are blessed to live lives that are clean and often 100 percent sober and 100 percent free from drugs, alcohol, pornography, adultery, gambling, stealing, or any other compulsive behavior that once dominated and controlled their lives. This sobriety may be the most cherished thing in a restored leader's life because they know that if they ever relapse, it's curtains.

Focused Leadership

When leaders are recovered from their failures, they have crystal-clear thinking and usually make razor-sharp decisions. It's amazing how focused and sharp a sober mind can be. Everyone around that leader can tell the difference because they were used to this leader operating below their ultimate capacity because they were making decisions while "high" on their own addictive behaviors and pride and arrogance. But once Humpty Dumpty falls, gets help around the causes of his fall, and gets back on the wall broken, his attention is keen and his judgment is clear and his focus is exactly where it needs to be organizationally. It's amazing to watch and experience.

A Closer Relationship with God and Self

One of the many gifts that comes from a leader's restoration from any level of moral failure is the blessing of greater self-awareness. Leaders get to know themselves so much better because they're no longer alienated from themselves by the reckless self-comforting behavior and choices. An even greater gift is the spiritual formation that often accompanies the restoration of a fallen leader. For many leaders became so accustomed to working day and night without a deep abiding trust in and relationship with God that the failure blessed them to hit so low that they landed on their knees in the presence of God. So, in my rendition of the Humpty Dumpty story, when Humpty Dumpty fell, he gathered himself up on his knees. Quite frankly that's as high as he ever needed to go again because from that place he could lead far better. Fallen leaders get to meet a God who doesn't love us just because we're able to perform well and lead well, but His love surrounds us when we are no longer fit to lead and have nothing to say and no accomplishments to present to him. What a gift.

The Gift of Transparency

Sharon Hersh in her book *The Last Addiction* says, "Hiding is the breeding ground of addiction." Every person who's fallen into a sinful lifestyle knows that this is true. Another amazing reward of a restored leader is the ability to come out of hiding—to live a life that is an open book. What a blessing it is to no longer have to hide your Internet search history, to no longer have to delete text messages and phone calls from your cell phone history, and to no longer have to secure your email or have secret phones and email addresses and have everything secured with pass codes. He who has nothing to hide, hides nothing. That's a freedom that's hard to describe—the rest of a stress-free life when it comes to worrying about being discovered.

One of the games that I played with friends as a child growing up in my neighborhood was Hide-and-Seek. If you're familiar with the game, you may remember that if there were ten people playing, one person would be chosen to be "It." And if you were "It," you had to turn your back away from the rest of the players, close your eyes, and count to twenty while the rest of the players ran and hid in different locations. If you weren't "It," you would run with your heart racing, panting for air, and desperately looking for a place where you would not be discovered. The irony is that sometimes you could see the person looking for you, but they couldn't see you. My heart is racing now, just remembering those moments. The goal was to hide and not be found. You waited for the moment when *someone else was found,* and you would then hear the words, "Olly, Olly, Oxen Free." That meant everyone was now free. You could come out of your hiding place and being discovered would not cause you any consequences.

Every leader who got caught hiding, was exposed, and went through a recovery process of healing and correction and restoration, now gets to live their life every day with the words "Olly, Olly, Oxen, Free" ringing over their heads. Sir/Ma'am, you are free. You have no need to hide, and you have nothing to hide. You've done the work; you are now free.

Final Words

I would never have picked a life's journey that included such a huge public failure, but I'm so grateful for the person it's made me. I have more focus now than ever before. I have a better marriage now than ever before. I'm a better father now than ever before. I'm more compassionate now than ever before. In fact, there is nothing in my life that I can't say that's not better now than it was several years ago when I blew it. I'm better off relationally, professionally, financially, spiritually, physically, domestically, emotionally, mentally, and any other "ly" that I can think of. And it's all because God in his infinite love extended unmerited grace to this broken soul. Thank You, Lord, for a second chance.

I *so* want that for you too. I wrote this book so that you could not just recover, but one day flourish. I pray that it has blessed you in ways that only God could accomplish.

APPENDIX 1

An acrostic "F.A.S.T.E.R." from *Pure Desire* by Ted Roberts describes the person in the process of relapse:

F: Forgetting Priorities; movement away from trusting God and more toward their circumstances, keeps secrets, less time with God.

A: Anxiety; undefined fear and draws energy from their emotions, replaying past negative thoughts over and over.

S: Speeding Up; conscious or unconscious focus on work, skipping meals, staying up late, increased sugar or caffeine, over-exercising.

T: Ticked Off: using anger as a way of numbing the pain.

E: Exhausted: loss of physical and emotional energy due to the over usage of anger, depression sets in, panic, confusion, hopelessness, sheer exhaustion.

R: Relapse; return to the place where they swore they would never return, becomes out of control and lost in the addiction.

APPENDIX 2

Restoration Process of Leaders

Are you aware of a leader who has fallen and needs help getting back up? Will you love them enough to wash their feet? Dallas Theological Seminary Professor Bill Lawrence says that "Foot washing is really helping people clean up the messes that they've made along the journey of their lives." Restoring fallen leaders requires the courage to confront and the compassion to humbly wash feet. It takes a love and hope to want them to win again, and it *will* take time. I recommend a fourfold process of restoration:

1. **Rebuke and Discipline.** First of all the leader needs to be rebuked and corrected for their failure. To ignore a leader or brother or sister in the Lord, who has fallen into sin, is not loving. The Bible says that the people that God *loves* He disciplines and chastens and that if you are not disciplined and chastened by the Lord you are an illegitimate child. This rebuke doesn't always have to be public, but it should include a period of removal from actively carrying out the leader's position and function prior to their failure. Time frames will vary from person to person and situation to situation, but I suggest an indefinite period of time so that you don't put yourself on the hook and so that the person who's being disciplined doesn't just do what they have to do in the time frame needed and then get back in the game so-to-speak. I find that fallen leaders who have no specified time of returning to their leadership posts are more focused on healing than returning to leadership.

2. **Repentance and Support.** During the leader's season of discipline, there should be clear evidence of *repentance* from their sin or their poor decision making. In other words, they must acknowledge that what they were doing or saying was *wrong* first of all. It can't just be, "My pastor or bishop or Corporate thinks I was wrong." No, they must understand that what they were doing was wrong, and they must actively and sincerely turn away from their sin and break ties with all that they may have been immorally involved with. Repentance is significant. They're also going to need *support* during this time, primarily from others who may have walked down a similar road of failure but who are on the road of victory and righteousness now. They need to get involved regularly in support groups that deal with their sin of choice. You can't heal in isolation. God has placed healing in the Body. God will forgive your sins (1 John 1:9), but in order to heal, it must be brought into the light of loving spiritual community (James 5:16).

3. **Recovery and Change of Behavior.** I personally think that being sober and clean for about ninety days is a good foundation point to consider restoring a person. By then, the person has had temptations to relapse back into their old ways, and if they've been working their recovery program well, they've also been learning methods and tools to stay clean and free from whatever caused them to be set down. If they have truly been recovering and healing well, they will be better suited to return to leadership at this point than they've ever been in the past because they'll return broken, and that's a great place to serve from.

4. **Restoration and Recall.** After warning and preparing His disciples repeatedly concerning His pending arrest and execution and resurrection three days later, each one of Jesus' disciples not only forgot what He said, but they rebuked and didn't believe others when they told them that He had come back from the dead. Yet in spite of their disbelief and failure to remain faithful to Him, He rebuked them and then *re-called* them into His great service. As I wrote in chapter 6 it feels like being a benchwarmer on a sports team who never gets in the game because of repeated turnovers and mistakes you've made in the past, and yet at some point the coach calls your name and says, "Johnson, check in." And with

utter shock, you head into the game, amazed that the coach is giving you another chance. I don't believe failure is final, and I don't believe that once you've failed, God is finished using you. In fact, I *know* that's not the case, because if it was, I wouldn't be writing this book—I'm exhibit A, that God can and will recall you after you've failed. After you've been rebuked and disciplined and after you have repented and gotten lots of support from others who can relate to your failure and struggle and after you have recovered and changed your behavior and choices, God *will* restore you and recall you.

NOTES

1. Fortune Magazine estimates that "Companies experience an average shareholder loss of two hundred twenty-six million dollars in the three days after the announcement of a CEO indiscretion." http://fortune.com/2015/04/14/ceo-indiscretions-cost/?utm_content=buffer3f45aandutm_medium=socialandutm_source=twitter.comandutm_campaign=buffer
2. (Worthy of Her Trust by Arterburn and Martinkus).
3. (http://www.nbcnews.com/id/16099971/ns/technology_and_science-games/t/does-game-violence-make-teens-aggressive/#.U6NYyih7Tao

Biography

Keith Battle is married to his best friend, Vicki, and they have three adult children. He is the Senior Pastor of Zion Church. The church has locations in Landover, MD, Woodbridge, VA, and Fort Washington, MD. He is also the creator of a radio sports minute called, "When Sports Meet Life", and can also be heard on the weekly radio broadcast, "Weekly Wisdom". Keith is an Executive Consultant for church and business leaders and is a regular NBA & NFL Chapel Speaker. For more information, bookings, or other products available by Keith Battle, visit sagacity-company.com

CPSIA information can be obtained at www.ICGtesting.com
Printed in the USA
BVOW06s1815260416

445678BV00016B/74/P